BURPEE AMERICAN GARDENING SERIES

CONTAINER GARDENING

BURPEE

AMERICAN GARDENING SERIES

CONTAINER GARDENING

Suzanne Frutig Bales

PRENTICE HALL GARDENING

New York ◆ *London* ◆ *Toronto* ◆ *Sydney* ◆ *Tokyo* ◆ *Singapore*

To my eldest son, Tom Meacham, who has brought me great joy and happiness.

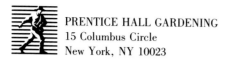

PRENTICE HALL GARDENING
15 Columbus Circle
New York, NY 10023

Library of Congress Cataloging-in-Publication Data

Bales, Suzanne Frutig.
    Container gardening / Suzanne Frutig Bales.
        p.   cm.—(Burpee American gardening series)
    Includes index.
    ISBN 0-671-84648-5
    1. Container gardening.   I. Title.   II. Series.
SB418.B35   1993
635.9'86—dc20   92-6021
                             CIP

I would like to thank the many people who provided me with unending help, support and love while I wrote this book: my husband and best friend, Carter F. Bales, my father and unofficial editor, Edward C. Frutig, my gardening partner Martha Kraska, my research assistant Gina Norgard and Alice Recknagel Ireys, my close friend and mentor.

I would like to thank the experts who shared their knowledge: Connie and Jim Cross, J. Barry Ferguson, Rudolph D. Nabel, Kathy Pufahl, and Marco Polo Stufano. Thank you to the garden designers who provided inspiration as well as allowed me to photograph their designs: Denise Puccinelli, Connie Cross, Diane Sjoholm, Tish Rehill, Rosalind Creasy and Adele S. Mitchel. Thanks also to the many people whose gardens I photographed: Mr. and Mrs. Francis H. Cabot, Elizabeth F. Failing, J. Barry Ferguson, Katharine Heyes, Alice and Richard Netter, and J. Liddon Pennock, Jr. Several gardens open to the public graciously allowed me to photograph their designs: Callaway Gardens, Wave Hill Botanical Garden and Old Westbury Gardens. I am indebted to the Burpee staff: Chela Kleiber, Barbara Wolverton and Elda Malgieri.

Photography credits: Agricultural Research Service, USDA: pp. 92–93; Ball Seed Co.: p. 24 bottom right; Druse, Ken: pp. 6, 13 bottom left, 14 bottom left, 33 bottom right, 42; Kraska, Martha: p. 10 bottom left; Mehling, Joseph: p. 24 top; Rokach, Allen: pp. 17 bottom left, 39 top right, 51 left; W. Atlee Burpee & Co.: pp. 14 right, 45 left, 49 top, 51 right, 52 left, 53, 55 bottom right, 76, 86; Woodyard, Cynthia: pp. 27 top left, 38 left, 39 top left, 49 middle, 58 bottom, 59, 61 top left, 69 top, 80. **Line drawings:** Michael Gale except drawings on pages 16, 23 and 72 courtesy of W. Atlee Burpee & Co.

Designed by Patricia Fabricant and Levavi & Levavi
Manufactured in the United States of America

10 9 8 7 6 5 4 3 2 1

First Edition

Cover: *Kathy Heyes plants for fragrance and beauty in her containers, combining the sweet scents of heliotrope and petunias with Marguerite daisies and the silvery licorice plant.*

Preceding pages: *This terrace was designed with pockets between the stones to hold plants. Containers are randomly grouped on a terrace to give the feeling of a full garden.*

CONTENTS

INTRODUCTION

Many a transformation from barren city terrace to tropical jungle is at the hands of an overzealous gardener who discovers it's nearly impossible to find a spot where a container planting won't fit. Pots come in all sizes and shapes, for standing on the ground, sitting on tables and hanging on walls, but pots aren't the only containers. This book discusses plants held in "contained" spaces, and with definite boundaries, such as pockets of soil between paving stones and in stone walls.

The number of plants suitable for growing in containers is greater than the selection of appropriate containers. For the curious, container gardening soon becomes an opportunity for exploration. A container can enhance the already beautiful and camouflage the eyesore. A single, simple pot of flowers can be the finishing touch, lending its warmth and beauty to the area it decorates. In addition, if carefully chosen, the flowers will perfume the air. Flowers in containers pop up in the most unexpected places. In Lake Placid, New York, I saw them arranged on either side of the municipal parking meters. Hats off to the city planner. How could one not wish to park there, even at the risk of staying a little too long and getting a ticket? In another resort town, window boxes built into either side of their wooden trash containers turned an area of ugly necessity into a beautiful asset. The entrances of toll booths on many throughways say "welcome" with flowers. Even the dreary tunnels that lead into New York City are decorated with containers filled with annuals—beautiful despite their surroundings. Many shops across America have window boxes and hanging baskets full of flowers decorating their entrances, inviting customers inside. The San Francisco Wharf imaginatively combines lesser-known annuals, perennials and vines in oversized containers to provide a garden walkway. A gas station in my hometown is smothered with flowers, some even hanging from the gas pumps. There are window boxes on the station house, and several giant sunflowers, like superior beings, hold court in the parking area; it puts a whole new perspective on filling your tank.

Pots of blooming flowers are enticing mood changers. With flowers, an austere entrance or sparsely decorated terrace or balcony can become cozy and inviting. A quite ordinary house in an area where all houses are similar can sparkle and charm the passerby with a window box or pots of flowers on the porch. I've often wanted to stop and thank the owners for the pleasure they give.

Don't despair if you haven't room for a garden. You certainly have room for a container or two, and, large or small, they spread the joy of growing. But remember, the vitality of a container garden depends on your curiosity and energy. This is what makes the difference between a good garden and a mediocre one.

This book is meant to guide you through the principles of designing and growing plants in containers. There is information on how to group containers together into gardens and how to group plants from different classifications in the same container. Vines, annuals and houseplants all can be combined in a large container. Skim through the pages and enjoy the many photographs. They will help you envision possibilities and acquaint you with unfamiliar plants and new combinations. The needs of hundreds of plants are treated in depth in the plant portrait chapters of other books in the *Burpee American Gardening Series*. This book will get you started, with guidelines to help you, but there are no rigid rules. You are the designer, and your taste prevails.

Working with the vast and ever-growing number of plants that can be combined in containers is an exploration in design and beauty. Because plants are endlessly unfolding their mysteries, there are results you and I can't predict but can only discover. No matter how many containers we fill, a lifetime isn't long enough to explore all the possibilities.

Overflowing with plants and trees (all grown in containers), an apartment terrace designed and planted by Victor Nelson creates a sense of tropical lushness and provides privacy and beauty unexpectedly amid surrounding city buildings.

THE CONTAINER PLANNER

The most obvious locations for container plantings are terraces, decks, balconies, porches and roof tops where gardens are not practical. Usually the containers are grouped, if there is more than one, at floor level. However, containers can do much more than stand at your feet in the expected places. They can be your personal troop of entertainers, hostesses and decorators. If they are placed at the front door, they offer friendly greetings as they invite the visitor in. Hanging from porch ceilings, they are trapeze artists. On stairways they guide the way up, and at the entrance to a garden they announce to visitors where the garden begins. As decorators they beautify windows, soften the edges of walks, and camouflage austere walls.

PLACEMENT

Clustered together, containers create a portable garden, an easy way to decorate different areas at different times, or the same area in different ways. They dress up an otherwise drab location. When placed around the perimeter of a garden they expand it. They can serve as a dividing wall between two areas, or as a screen to block an unattractive view. They provide movement with graceful transition from one area to another—a procession of containers can lead the eye up steps, around corners, along the tops of walls and into doorways, or bring the movement to a halt by directing the eye to a focal point. An individual container placed in the center of a garden or otherwise standing alone draws attention to itself just as a piece of sculpture would.

Existing structures can be used as containers, too. Stone walls can have plants poked into the little pockets of soil between the stones. Cracks between bricks or slate on a terrace make ideal planters where the plant roots spread out under the stones. The stones act as a mulch, keeping the roots cool in summer and warm in winter, all the while holding in moisture. Even crevices only a few inches deep can be planted.

We tend to use flowers in pots to grace our living spaces, but I readily admit to placing planters in a garden border to hide a less-than-graceful plant, to prop up those fallen from grace, or to cover bare ground. (They also keep the weeds from growing until I replant.) Call it cheating if you will, but for me, anything that improves the look of a garden helps to make it more enjoyable. Use every trick available to create a place of beauty. If eyesores exist in the garden, they distract from the overall beauty—the rotten apple that can spoil the barrel.

At Calloway Gardens in Pine Mountain, Georgia, a window box's flower colors are coordinated not only with one another but with the red window frame as well. Red salvia, yellow 'Lemon Gem' marigold, silvery dusty miller and white-flowering periwinkle all combine for a full and attractive look.

CONTAINERS CELEBRATING THE SEASONS

Plantings in containers can be changed to celebrate the seasons. Some plants themselves change with the seasons, the perennial sedum 'Autumn Joy' and the shrub hydrangea, for example. Both of these change color and are interesting almost year 'round. In the spring sedum 'Autumn Joy' sprouts green succulent leaves and stems. The early flowers are also green, looking a little like broccoli florets, but as summer progresses they change from green to pink to rose. The cool fall weather continues the process, and the rose flowers change to red, and finally to deep rust. The flower heads dry naturally and remain all winter to catch the falling snow. Similarly, hydrangeas hold their fluffy flower heads through many seasons as they change color from pink, white, blue or green to various shades of brown.

Favorite combinations, which can be repeated year after year, will add to your holiday enjoyment. Placing planting pots within decorative pots makes a quick make-over, an easy way to celebrate a holiday or herald a new season with the appropriate flowers. The plants themselves, if full enough, will hide the edges of the container. Moss can be used, too, to make containers even more attractive, concealing the fact that one pot is sitting in another. Both Spanish and decorator moss are available from nurseries and florists, and depending on the look you want, both work well. Spanish moss grows in silvery strands that are easily separated and fluffed to drape on top of bare

The same container gives a very different effect when planted differently each season. Through the years the pair of cement planters at the entrance to the author's house have featured a variety of seasonal looks. Top left: *In spring Johnny-jump-ups or pansies are planted to complement the tulips that line the walk.* Top right: *In summer, a standard white rosebush blooms over ivy and alyssum.* Bottom left: *Ornamental kale planted in early fall is not harmed until a prolonged freeze; the plants stay until just before Christmas, when live pines are planted.* Bottom right: *The pines remain in the planters until spring, when they are transplanted to another part of the property and the cycle of seasonal planting begins again.*

soil and over the container's rim. Decorator moss is green and comes in flat pieces that can be cut to any size.

A large permanent container can be planted with a variety of plants that will bloom at different seasons. Spring bulbs announce the first change in season of each new year, and they can either be planted in outdoor containers in the fall or purchased in bud to bloom in the spring and move into place. Crocuses, daffodils and tulips are the easiest and the most reliable of spring bulbs to grow. They need only a small space, just their size. Their threadlike roots grow no more than a few inches and don't interfere with the growth of neighboring plants. Daffodils and tulips can be planted deeper than the six inches usually recommended, so that other, smaller bulbs, annuals and perennials can be planted directly above them. Layered in this way, a container can be fully packed so it won't look sparse; the stems of the bulbs will easily find their way up, around and through the plants on top.

In milder zones (Zone 6 and south) an evergreen shrub in a container can be surrounded by layers of spring bulbs. Try tulips or daffodils in the bottom layer (planted 6 inches deep, with at least another 2 inches of soil beneath them), squills or blue puschkinias in the middle layer (4 inches deep), and snowdrops and crocuses in the top layer (2 inches deep). When the weather warms in the spring, seeds of alyssum can be sprinkled on the bare soil between the bulbs to bloom in five to six weeks' time and continue blooming all summer into the fall. If the bulbs are closely planted and are to return the following year, it could be difficult to plant established annuals around them, but alyssum is shallow-rooted and will not disturb the bulbs. If only larger bulbs, daffodils and tulips, are planted, they can be planted deeper than usual, up to 10 inches deep, and annuals can easily be planted on top after the bulbs have finished blooming without digging deep enough to hurt the bulbs.

Long-blooming primroses and pansies like cool nights and are not bothered by light frost. They can be added to a container in the spring, tucked in around bulbs or under a spring-flowering shrub, to extend the bloom for many weeks. Forsythia, azalea and flowering almond are good spring-flowering shrubs for underplanting. After they finish blooming, the primroses can be transplanted and a summer-blooming flower planted in their place. (The primroses can be permanently planted out into a garden, yours or a friend's, where they will return each spring thereafter for many years. The pansies will not return and are added to the compost heap.)

By far the largest variety of flowers is available in May and June, when the gardener, with his many choices, is constrained only by the money in his pocket. The most popular flowers for summer are impatiens, geraniums and petunias. Larger containers can hold roses or other summer-blooming shrubs. The quick growth and abundance of flowers characteristic of May and June lead us to the slow droop of July, a time when no matter how skilled the gardener, some plants will succumb to heat, drought or pests. If pests grab a plant when you're not looking, replacement and recovery can also be quick. A few pots can be moved to hide the loss, or a new plant can be transplanted into its place.

Fall's cooling breezes bring renewed energy and spurts of growth. Plants perk up for a bit, before the disarray of autumn is apparent as plants spill over onto one another. Many plants that love cool nights come into their own in the fall. Nasturtiums, roses and petunias send out full, overblown blooms after spending a number of quiet, less productive weeks in the high heat of summer. Chrysanthemums, flowering kale, cabbage, lettuce and ornamental peppers will bloom through frosty nights and keep containers bright.

Where winters are short and mild, Zones 7 and 8, and the warmer areas of Zone 6 (see the information regarding winter protection, page 77), many evergreens are at home in containers even with freezing winter temperatures; they keep the terrace, balcony or walkway alive in winter as they sparkle when covered with snow. The bare branches of some shrubs, among them red twig dogwood (*Cornus sanguinea*) and the twisted branches of Harry Lauder's walking stick (*Corylus avellava* 'Contorta'), are beautiful without leaves. In the more northern zones, 6 through 3, permanent all-weather containers and window boxes can be filled with cut branches of various evergreens poked into the soil and arranged to create a tapestry of green that will be decorative and look handsome for many months.

A GARDEN OF CONTAINERS

Potted plants grouped together create a garden—a movable garden, one in which the elements can be rearranged like furniture in a room. Anything that can be grown in a garden can be grown in a container garden. The owner of a small yard doesn't have to worry about losing his garden if he puts in a terrace, because a terrace can hold a container garden.

What would you like? You can indeed have it all. Choosing a theme for your container garden can add another dimension of interest and help you to be more creative. Is it to be a garden of fragrance, where the aroma of flowers can be enjoyed up close, or a moonlight garden, lighting the evening terrace with the glow of white flowers that reflect the moonlight? Consider a sunset garden, bold with the exuberant reds, oranges and yellows of the setting sun. Perhaps an old-fashioned garden planted with the flowers your grandmother loved is more suited to your temperament. Maybe a practical salad garden by the kitchen door would suit you better. Even a perennial garden and a cutting garden can be grown in containers. The impact of a garden can't be judged by its size. Size has nothing to do with success. Gardens and dreams grow together. I have seen a very productive cutting garden grown in a rectangular wooden planter, 2 feet by 4 feet, situated at the edge of a balcony.

Container gardens can sprawl across terraces, rise vertically to create partitions and hang from trellises or walls. Pedestals, tables, tree stumps and plant stands are a few ways to move plants up off the ground, so that they take up very little floor space.

A plant stand can be placed like a screen to hide a private area, to divide one space from another, or to brighten a barren wall. The advantages of having plants at different levels are many. Furry plants can be petted. The aroma of fragrant plants can be savored. Details of dainty plants can be seen easily, and plants set at a higher level can be cared for without bending over. An elderly or handicapped person can work comfortably seated if container plantings can be set within arm's reach.

When grouping containers together, a garden feeling can be achieved if the containers are arranged to form a geometric shape. Almost any geometric shape is pleasing. A crescent or quarter moon, half circle,

At John Gardener's tennis ranch in Carmel, California, large flower borders of containers surround the many gazebos and terraces. The gardens are changed four times a year to celebrate the seasons. Of course it takes planning, money and hard work to keep pots of flowers waiting in the wings, but the gardens are always in full bloom as containers are replaced when their flowers fade.

This terrace was planned for container gardens with pockets of soil left open for planting between the stones. The in-ground plants and the containers of plants complement each other. Ivy, trained like a hedge, makes a dark background that shows off the containers.

Container Kits

There are container kits available that allow many plants to be grown in a small area. The most popular kits featured in the Burpee catalog are the patio tower gardens. Covering an area 2 feet square and raised 4 feet high, each tower features long-lasting redwood slats in 46-foot-long wraparound rows for growing flowers, lettuce, herbs and strawberries. It is filled with 4½ cubic feet (112.5 quarts) of lightweight planting mix. The base is rot-resistant plywood fitted with heavy-duty casters for turning or moving. An interior reservoir fills easily from the top and allows water and fertilizer to seep gradually to the plants' roots. (The garden tower is also available in a 2-foot-high size that can be turned into a "strawberry bush" when planted with 50 strawberry plants. It holds about 2¼ cubic feet of soil and has 26 feet of planting rows.) Patio tower gardens can be planted permanently with perennial plants and left out all winter.

A small garden at the edge of a pool is enlarged when bordered with three pots of pink petunias and one pot of blue lobelias. It is easy to add different flowers for each season.

Chimney-flue tiles are arranged together to form an island of plants leading to a barn at Calloway Gardens in Pine Mountain, Georgia. The bottomless flues are set on a mulched path which provides good drainage.

Plantings of pink and purple petunias, repeated in three round containers, border the larger matched pair of square containers which overflow with heliotrope, Marguerite daisies and silver Helichrysum petiolatum. The sweet vanilla fragrance of the heliotrope scents the air for the pleasure of all who sit on the terrace.

A reflecting pool at the edge of a terrace becomes a water garden when surrounded by pots of flowers. From the cherub clockwise around the pool are pots of dipladenia, lantana, purple petunia, cupflower (Nierembergia hippomanica violacea), browallia, blue daisy (Felicia amelloides), yellow begonia, verbena, variegated ivy and orange clivia.

Ken Druse artfully clustered together potted plants on a rooftop to create a garden as beautiful as any planted in the ground. His pots contain a mixture of annuals, perennials and bulbs.

A patio tower garden® kit covers only 2 feet of space but provides 46 feet of rows wrapped around the sides of the pyramid for planting flowers or vegetables. An interior reservoir is filled from the top and allows water and fertilizer to seep gradually to the plants' roots. Such kits are available at many nurseries and can also be ordered from the Burpee catalog.

rectangle, square, triangle and oval are the most common. It can even be an island to walk around or a corner of the terrace. To create a container garden, arrange the plants within the "garden" shape according to their height. Generally, the tallest plants should be placed at the back, unless the garden is meant to be walked around, in which case they belong in the middle. It is never wise, nor is it particularly interesting, to follow rules of height and design rigidly. A tall plant moved to the front or a short plant in the back elevated, on top of an upside-down pot or two, adds an interesting twist to the placement of the containers.

Hanging Baskets

Flowers in all their beauty should be looked up to, and hanging baskets allow just that as they elevate them for display. Don't be timid. Hang plants like pictures on outdoor walls, gazebos, trellises, fences and railings. Dangle them from porch ceilings, like chandeliers, and float them overhead any place you can screw in a hook. Even lamp-lights perk up with a hanging basket of flowers as a frill at their necks.

Trees are unexpected places to decorate with hanging bas-kets. One garden I visited years ago had eleven hanging baskets filled with shade-loving plants—begonias, impatiens and ivy—hanging from the lower branches encircling a tree. One side of the tree held a hammock and the other a small table and chairs. It made an enchanting place for a meal.

In early summer, hanging baskets are inviting places for birds to nest. Many years ago, while reading the morning pa-per on the porch, I noticed a purple finch building a nest in a hanging basket of ivy gerani-ums. As I watched fascinated at the bird's progress and choice of materials, I realized I had to make a decision. Would I al-low the finch to keep its nest and sacrifice the geranium, or should I move the nest now? I simply let it be. When the plant needed watering I couldn't sit and let it suffer, so I gently lifted it down and watered around the nest. The mother finch never seemed to mind. She flew away when I approached and resumed her seat when I left. We watched the eggs hatch, the babies being fed and finally the young ones leave the nest. As we didn't touch the nest, the eggs or the baby birds, the mother bird didn't seem to object. Every year since, at least one finch nest and sometimes as many as four have been built, each in a dif-ferent hanging basket around our porch. The plants that grew were beautifully lush, probably from all the added fertilizer the birds contributed. Because the plants were so full, visitors never no-ticed the nests unless I pointed them out. So you see, hanging

A porch is changed into a garden room with individual hanging baskets of ivy, geraniums and ferns. Dipladenia vines in planters at the base of the posts grow up the trellis.

ARCHING PLANTS FOR HANGING BASKETS

COMMON NAME	LATIN NAME
Angel-wing begonia	*Begonia corallina* 'Elaine' or 'Orange Rubra'
Cherry tomato	'Basket King' or 'Basket Pak'
Flowering maple	*Abutilon* 'Moonchimes'
Impatiens	*Impatiens wallerana, I. Schlecteri*
Ivy geranium	*Pelargonium peltatum*
Ivy	*Hedera* species
Lady's-eardrop	*Fuchsia* species
Shrub verbena*	*Lantana* species
Spider plant	*Chlorophytum comosum* 'Vittatum'
Wandering Jew	*Tradescantia fluminensis*

TRAILING PLANTS FOR WIRE BASKETS

COMMON NAME	LATIN NAME
Creeping thyme*	*Thymus serpyllum*
Lobelia	*Lobelia erinus*
Miniature ivy	*Hedera* species
Nasturtium*	*Tropaeolum majus*
Pennyroyal*	*Mentha pulegium*
Sweet alyssum*	*Lobularia maritima*

VINES FOR HANGING BASKETS

COMMON NAME	LATIN NAME
Black-eyed Susan vine	*Thunbergia alata*
Bougainvillea	*Bougainvillea glabra*
Moonflower*	*Ipomoea alba*
Morning glory	*Ipomoea* species
Passionflower*	*Passiflora* species

*Fragrant plants

In areas with cool nights like Jackson Hole, Wyoming, pansies last all summer. This photograph was taken in mid-August, and the pansies are still blooming as though it were spring. White petunias and deep, bluish purple and white alyssums spill from the basket, and the sparse blooms of cosmos peek out at the back. The soil in the hanging pot is too fertile for the cosmos to flower profusely, but it produces lush green foliage that is attractive without flowers, and frames the bold shapes of the petunias.

TOMATO HANGING BASKET

One tomato plant in a hanging basket will provide a nice harvest within a hand's reach.

baskets can serve many purposes, from functioning as birdhouses to being purely decorative.

When planting a hanging basket, it is important to locate the plants to balance your pot so that it will hang straight. A rule of thumb is two or three properly placed plants to a 6-inch basket, three or four to an 8-inch basket. Remember that we look up at hanging baskets, and they aren't attractive if what we view is only a bare bottom. The most successful plants for hanging baskets are the "weeping" plants whose stems have a branching and softly arching habit of draping over the edges and down the sides of the pot like a water fountain. If an upright, single-stemmed plant is used, it will resemble a rocket ship soaring toward the sky instead of falling gracefully down toward the viewer.

Vines are a good choice for hanging baskets. They can clamber around the suspension wires and up to the ceiling or fall over the edges to hang in plaits down the sides (see page 61 for more on vines). To ensure that as the plant grows it graces all the sides of the container, 6-inch-long hairpins can be placed gently over the stems and into the soil to train them in place.

Wire hanging baskets are a bit more complicated to plant than solid baskets, but they are worth the effort. They allow plants to grow out of the bottom of the container to give a rounded and fully groomed appearance. The inside of the basket is lined with a sheet of dampened sphagnum moss, with the green side placed toward the wire. Position the largest piece of moss first in the basket. Not only will it live longer but it will hold the soil better than smaller

pieces overlapped. Depending on where the wire basket will hang, you might want to line the back of the moss (the soil side) with black plastic sheeting for extra protection against drying out and to prevent excess dripping if the planter is overwatered. Small, shallow-rooted, trailing plants that will grow out the bottom of the container are added next. They will be easier to add if the roots are gently washed clean of soil before they are inserted into the moss. Make a slit with a sharp knife through the plastic into the moss and insert the roots. Once they are in place, a good lightweight potting soil should be placed around and between the roots; spread the roots out as they are covered with soil. Next, larger plants can be planted to circle the sides. Fill the container to an inch or two below the rim. Now add the top plants, with the tallest in the center and the plants with a more trailing habit around the edge. Firm the potting soil around each plant and water gently. Additional moss can be added between the top plants to act as a mulch and slow evaporation. Some wire baskets have a flat side for hanging flush with a wall. The difference when planting flat-sided baskets is that you put the tallest plant at the back, and there is one less side to plant.

For hanging baskets, it is important that you select plants that prefer to dry out between waterings. A hanging basket will dry out more quickly than any other container because both its base and sides are surrounded by drying air. Frequently it is more exposed to the sun. On dry, hot days, soil additives and peat moss are especially useful in helping to hold water. On the hottest days, plants in direct sun may need water both in the morning and the evening. Furthermore, all of this additional watering will leach the nutrients out of the soil, and it is important to fertilize. The plants, if forgotten, will certainly tell you with a droop if they need attention. Most are forgiving and resilient if forgotten only once or twice, but if neglected regularly, they will lose their luster and their will to live.

Too much water can also be a problem, especially if the hanging basket will be where rainwater can fill and drench it. Drainage holes are essential in hanging baskets. Saucers are available with many hanging baskets to catch water overflow,

Foliage plants give a peaceful and quiet mood to a shady gazebo. The towers of varigated ivy with their green leaves splashed with white mimic the dappled sunlight that sparkles through the trellis, and the ferns add softness. This is a cool and delightful spot for an afternoon drink or a quiet place to read the daily paper.

An antique horse head, no longer needed to tether horses, is an ideal place to hang a pot of lantana.

Lampposts need not be bare. Dress them with hanging baskets of ivy, geranium and vinca.

so these baskets are useful for areas where dripping water would be a nuisance. The wind may swing the plant, so that the roots will grow less deeply, more laterally, than if the same plant were on the ground.

Window Boxes and Wall Hangers

The charm of window boxes can't be overestimated. Window boxes soften rigid lines, breaking up the expanse of a barren wall with the grace of flowers. They do double duty, overflowing with flowers that brighten the view from inside your house while they add color to the exterior view. Window boxes have long been a tradition in Europe, from the great cities to even the smallest villages. There

they are a necessity many wouldn't be without. In Holland, Switzerland and England, window boxes are frequently planned as part of the architecture.

The boxes can be coordinated with the color of the house's trim. Painted the same color as the building, the effect is to draw more attention to the plants themselves. The flower colors should also be coordinated with the building and can echo the color of the trim or complement it. Not every window on one side of a house has to have a

Cherry tomatoes in a hanging basket can be practical as well as decorative, especially if grown near the kitchen.

Surrounded by plants, a gazebo at Meadowbrook Farm becomes a garden room. Hanging baskets of pink wax begonias, white impatiens, fuchsias and miniature ivy are overhead, and pots of geraniums, yellow tuberous begonias, ferns and tropical plants stand below. A standard variegated-leaf, red geranium is a vertical accent that joins the picture of the hanging plants and the plants on the ground.

window box. Just a single window box can add to the charm of the house. Plant each box bearing the window exposure in mind. Depending on whether the window gets sun or shade, it may be necessary to put different plants in each box. This can be very pretty, especially on an informal house where the effect can be reminiscent of a cottage garden. A more formal house usually requires a certain balance, most easily achieved by repeating the same plants in each box.

Flowers that do well in hot, dry locations (among them nasturtium, vinca, ivy geranium and lantana) are good choices for the South and for northern summers where the heat stays through the night. Many silver- or gray-leaved, felted or furry-leaved plants also enjoy the hot sun and dry conditions. These include dusty miller, lavender, licorice plant (*Helichrysum peliolatum*), lamb's ears, rosemary and many other herbs. Window boxes tend to be hot, dry locations for plants, especially in the sun, and these plants are good choices.

Practical and useful when placed outside a kitchen window, window boxes are a good place to plant herbs or a combination of herbs and edible flowers. This is a convenient location to harvest plants as needed for flavoring or garnishing foods. Even a salad garden can be grown in a window box.

*A window box painted the same color as the side of the store front doesn't distract from the beauty of pink petunia, scented geranium, blue cupflower (*Nierembergia caerulea*), silver dusty miller and gracefully draping ivy.*

White impatiens light up a shady window box. Ivy trained as a standard and precisely placed in the center of the window adds a formality that nicely contrasts with the whimsy of an ornamental peacock casually peeking out.

Petunias and purple lobelias spill from a window box, brightening the outside of the author's house from late spring until long after fall frost.

Where foundation plantings aren't possible, buildings can be dressed with window boxes. The window boxes don't have to be attached to the buildings. Planted with the same flowers (blue salvias, rose geraniums, heliotrope, swan river daisies and dahlberg daisies), these three white planters decorate the base of a summer house.

Window boxes can be placed directly on window sills or attached to walls under windows. It is important that they be safely and securely attached to prevent a strong wind or their own weight from knocking them down. The higher the window box is from the ground, the longer it will escape the ravages of light frost and the longer the flowers will bloom. Usually soil in window boxes will dry out sooner than ground soil because, as in hanging baskets, it is more exposed to the sun and drying wind. Avoid planting tall varieties in an exposed area where they may be hurt by the wind. If a trellis can be attached around a window, flowering vines can be trained to wreath a window with ribbons of color. Some vines, ivy and climbing hydrangea, for example, will cling to any surface. It isn't necessary to add a trellis for them; just prune them into the shape you want. If the vines start to grow over the window, trim them or tie them as you train them to grow on the wall. Strings can be secured from a window box to a balcony above or below, or to a drainpipe, or to an overhang, to provide a path for those vines that twist to climb along. Finally, a window isn't necessary as an excuse to hang flowers on the wall. Half-round baskets made of wire, plastic or terra-cotta can be arranged like pictures in groups or singly.

Strawberry Pots

Strawberry pots, taller than they are wide, are studded with numerous pockets around their sides. Usually made of terra-cotta, they were originally designed for growing many strawberry plants in a small space. Over the years I have tried growing different plants in strawberry pots, and it took me a long time to discover the obvious: Strawberries are the easiest plants to grow in strawberry pots. Plants in a strawberry pot need more attention than they do in a single pot, as care must be taken to see that each plant growing from the numerous openings receives enough sun and water, but they are well worth the extra effort.

Planting a strawberry pot is complicated but not difficult. Put an inch or two of gravel, Styrofoam peanuts or broken pottery in the bottom. Fill the pot with a good potting soil to just below the first opening in the side. If you are using started plants, it is best to wash the soil gently off the roots. This will make it easier to poke them through the openings into the pot. As always, take care with bare-root plants; keep from direct sunlight and replant them as quickly as possible. Slip the roots through the opening with one hand and reach into the pot from the top opening with your other hand to spread the roots out over the soil. Next, cover the roots with soil and firm it gently in place. Add more soil as you continue turning the pot and planting each opening. When you reach the top of the pot, plant the opening and water gently. Water and a little soil will probably spill out from each opening until the plants are more established and their roots hold the soil in place.

When choosing plants other than strawberry plants (strawberry plants are especially tough), remember that the plants at the bottom will have to be the most tolerant. Their roots will grow under the weight of the soil and the other plants above them. Any plant that is happy growing in a rock wall will like living in a strawberry pot.

To grow thirsty plants in a strawberry pot, place a water reservoir in the center of the pot. It is a more complicated process to plant a strawberry pot this way, but the pot will require less maintenance later. When the coarse drainage material is in place at the bottom of the pot, a piece of plastic drainage pipe or an old garden hose pierced with multiple holes can be stood up in the center of the pot with its bottom pushed into the coarse material at the bottom. The pipe or hose must be tall enough to reach the top

---

PLANTS FOR STRAWBERRY POTS

COMMON NAME	LATIN NAME
Catnip	*Nepeta cataria*
Chive	*Allium* species
Creeping thyme	*Thymus serpyllum*
Hen and chicks	*Sempervivum* species
Ivy	*Hedera* species
Mint	*Mentha* species
Parsley	*Petroselinum* species
Pennyroyal	*Mentha pulegium*
Rosemary	*Rosmarinus officinalis*
Stonecrop	*Sedum* species
Strawberry	*Fragaria* × *Ananassa*
Sweet alyssum	*Lobularia maritima*

of the pot. As soil and plants are added to the pot, the pipe will be supported on all sides. The top of the pipe or hose should stand an inch above the soil to prevent soil from washing into the opening and plugging it. Moss or the draping foliage of plants will hide the opening. Filled with water, this pipe or hose will drain slowly into the surrounding soil, and the strawberry pot will require less frequent watering.

Larger Containers

The larger the container, whether it be a half barrel, tub, oversized pot or urn, the greater the variety of plants the gardener can choose from. Deciduous trees (dwarf ornamental or fruit), evergreens, shrubs, flowers and vegetables can all be grown in tubs, for example. Half barrels are the most readily available and the least expensive of the big containers. Informal in appearance, they can be spruced up considerably, even painted to coordinate with their surroundings.

If the container in question is to be viewed from all sides, one to three upright plants—their number depending on their size—should be placed in the center, with three to five cascading plants placed around the sides. Plants with a cascading habit will unify the look of the container while softening the arrangement. Vines are especially effective in container plantings, where they are the supporting actors to the stars. Short flowering vines or ivies are most commonly used, but beans, to-

Brimming with assorted succulents, a strawberry pot is raised off the ground by an another upside-down terra-cotta pot. Succulents are good plants for crowding into a pot. They have minimal needs, tolerating drought and poor nutrition, and will gladly share water and nutrients with their neighbors.

At Montgomery Place a newly planted strawberry pot sprouts moss rose (Portulaca grandiflora), a drought-tolerant annual that thrives in full sun and will grow bushy and bloom all summer.

The blue lobelia spilling out the sides of the strawberry pot complements the white impatiens growing on top. These plants combine to brighten a shady spot.

matoes and miniature pumpkins add unexpected beauty with their trailing growth draping down the side of a container rather than up a stake or trellis. Longer-lasting moonflowers and morning glories, usually trained up trellises, are entertaining when presented growing downward and spilling onto the ground.

The larger the container, the more important cascading plants become to "soften" the solid base and integrate the plants with the container. If all the plants in the container stand upright and the rim of the container is left showing, the strong contrast between plant and planter distracts from the pretty effect. This is to be avoided, unless, of course, the container is meant to be a showpiece in itself. In most cases the container is best left as a vehicle to display plants, something that should blend into the background.

Standards in Containers

A standard is a plant that has been trained, against its inclination, to grow in the shape of a tree; picture the shape of a lollipop. The standard is a basic design used in topiary. Once trained, standards are simple to maintain. Some of the easiest plants to train as standards include such herbs as lavender and rosemary. Various roses,

Today strawberry pots are infrequently planted with strawberries. The foliage of strawberry plants growing out of the pots' side pockets is attractive even before they flower and produce fruit. Sweet alyssum, seeded on the top, comes quickly into bloom in six to eight weeks. By summer's end it will be frothing over the top and well down the sides of the pot, scenting the air with its sweet fragrance.

Dress up half barrels with paint. In this photograph the discreetly painted, deep green barrels allow the colors of the variegated ivy, browallias and petunias to be the center of attention.

Large containers can be packed to overflowing with 'Nicki Hybrid' flowering tobacco if they are deep enough to allow the plants to stretch down their roots, and if they are regularly watered and fertilized.

shrubs and evergreens are also commonly used. If you want to train your own standard, select a young plant with only one strong, straight stem. As the plant grows, remove any branches that grow out of the bottom two-thirds of the stem. The idea is to train the plant to develop a trunk, or one strong stem, that will increase in girth as the plant ages. The growth of the standard depends on the plant selected, taking a season for herbs or geraniums, or years for boxwood.

There are many variations to the theme of the "lollipop" standard. Instead of a spherical top, try a mushroom, a cone or multiple balls of foliage (a sort of poodle design). A single stem could be swirled as it grows upward into a spiral. Three stems can be braided together. The topiary art form is simple in theory but sometimes complicated to execute. No matter what design you choose, it will take patience to achieve the desired effect. Topiary plants can be purchased already grown and shaped, requiring only regular clipping to maintain, but the fun is in the doing, and if you like the look, it certainly is worth the effort.

Wall Gardens

Growing plants vertically in a wall garden is a dramatic way to decorate a patio or rooftop. Vegetables and flowers will thrive in a vertical frame with the planting material held in place by chicken wire and plastic

sheeting. Seedlings planted into the frame through slits in the plastic grow to cover the sides and top completely.

Flowers excellent for wall gardens include sweet alyssum, fibrous begonia, coleus, dwarf impatiens (in semishade), the 'Nugget'™ marigold and portulaca. Vegetables include Burpee's garden cress 'Curlycress'™; loosehead lettuce, especially 'Green Ice'ᵛᴾ, 'Oak Leaf', 'Salad Bowl' and 'Ruby'; 'Extra Curled Dwarf' parsley; and New Zealand spinach. A wall garden with 'Cheery Nugget'™ marigolds on one side and assorted loosehead lettuce on the other, with some 'Curlycress'™ on top, not only looks attractive but supplies tasty greens for salads. After the loosehead lettuce has been harvested, that side of the garden can be replanted with flowers or coleus to keep it attractive for the rest of the growing season.

A handy wall garden size measures 2 feet high, 2 feet wide and 6 inches deep, with straight sides. Use a flat board, 2 by 2 feet, for the bottom, and 1-inch-square boards to outline the sides and top. Paint the lumber or treat it with a nontoxic wood preservative (not creosote) before nailing the frame together. Wrap the sides and bottom of the frame with heavy clear plastic, then enclose it with chicken wire (1-inch mesh). Leave the top open. Use a staple gun or tacks to attach the plastic and wire firmly in place. To prevent bulging, hook a medium-heavy strand of wire

Contrasting plants with different growing habits add to the beauty of a large container. Impatiens 'Hawaiian Pink' grows upright in a full, rounded shape, perfect for the center of this half barrel. The pink petunias, blue browallias and variegated wax begonias gracefully arch over the sides.

Morning glories tumble down the sides of an oversized pot and by summer's end will be scrambling across the terrace.

CONSTRUCTION OF A WALL GARDEN

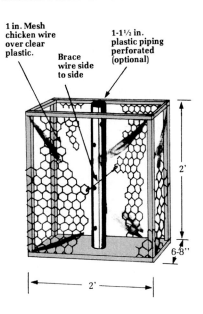

1 in. Mesh chicken wire over clear plastic.

Brace wire side to side

1-1½ in. plastic piping perforated (optional)

2'

6-8"

2'

In midsummer the front terrace to floral designer J. Barry Ferguson's house is decorated with living sculptures of ivy, herbs, shrubs and a standard red hibiscus. Ligustrum texanum *are trained into poodle shapes. Other planters with topiary herbs hold rosemary, lemon geranium and* Westringia rosmariniformis. *Blooming in the foreground is the variegated society garlic* (Tulbaghia violacea). *Window boxes of purple lantanas* (Lantana montevidensis) *and pots of pansies also provide spots of color.*

put it on a wheeled dolly, if you like.

Fill the frame from the top with a light, porous soil mixture. Water gently but thoroughly; let the mixture settle, add more mixture if necessary, and then water again before planting. Cut slits in the plastic with a sharp knife, in alternate openings in the wire mesh. Insert a small seedling—one with a pair of true leaves—in each slit, starting from the bottom and working up. Rooted cuttings of begonia and coleus can be used instead of seedlings for a faster "finished" effect. Firm the soil gently around the roots. Water the wall garden well after planting and continue to water as necessary, perhaps more than once a day in hot, sunny weather, much less often during a cool, cloudy spell. Shelter the wall garden from full sun and wind until

from side to side halfway between the top and bottom of the frame. Insert a piece of plastic piping (perforated with holes) in the center of the frame from top to bottom to facilitate watering. Decide where you want the wall garden before planting it, because it is almost impossible to move afterward; you can

When growing any plant as a standard remember to plant the base with a low-growing or draping plant to hide the soil. Pictured is a lantana standard underplanted with dusty miller.

Petunias are growing vertically in chicken-wire cages to create a wall of flowers.

the plants become established. If the light is not equal on all sides of the wall garden, turn it occasionally so plant growth will be uniform. If growth gets too thick and crowded, a plant here and there can be cut out; it's best to cut out rather than pull out a plant, as pulling may enlarge the hole in the plastic and allow soil and water to drip out.

PLANTS FOR PLANTING BETWEEN STONES

COMMON NAME	LATIN NAME
Basket-of-gold	*Aurinia saxatilis*
Catnip	*Nepeta cataria*
Creeping phlox	*Phlox subulata*
Hen and chicks	*Sempervivum tectorum*
Lavender	*Lavandula* species
Pennyroyal	*Mentha pulegium*
October plant	*Sedum sieboldii*
Stonecrop	*Sedum* species
Sweet alyssum	*Lobularia maritima*
Thyme	*Thymus* species

CONTAINERS IN THE GARDEN

Plants in containers can decorate a garden as well as a balcony or step. A container placed in the garden becomes a focal point. Even a small container can be an effective accent if placed in a border where it breaks up the monotony of perfectly defined plantings. A container in the garden can add height, interest, even an element of surprise. Gardens and their growth are unpredictable, and containers can be moved into a garden on the spur of the moment to camouflage an unsightly plant or to hide bare soil between plants.

Not all containers are pots and tubs. You can think of a raised garden bed as a permanent container. Whether used as a design feature to provide height, or as a corrective measure to improve the soil, a raised bed filled with top soil and compost provides ideal conditions for most plants. In a raised bed the soil warms faster, allowing the gardener to plant earlier; it also has better drainage and fewer weeds and provides more abundant flowers or vegetables.

Among the materials commonly used to build the retaining walls of a raised bed are railroad ties, logs (avoid creosote-treated wood) and stones. A raised bed should be constructed from 1 foot to 3 feet high, depending on whether the gardener wants to sit, kneel or stand while working. A 3-foot-high raised bed allows people confined to wheelchairs easy access to their garden and can bring many hours of pleasure and a satisfying feeling of accomplishment. When building a retaining wall, keep in mind that the bin (growing area) should be no wider than twice the distance you can reach. That way, you can work the bed from either side without having to stand on—and compress—the soil. A raised bed garden may consist of a single bed, a series of identical beds or a mix of variously geometric beds arranged to fit neatly into your growing area. Triangles, squares and even circles can be used effectively. Designed with various levels and planted with cascading plants to spill over the edges and down the sides, a raised bed can be a dramatic addition to a terrace or yard, adding dimension, interest and beauty, as well as ease of access, to the garden.

Rock gardens, like containers, have limited space for roots to grow. Old stone walls originally built as property-line markers or as foundations for buildings (usually barns) are ideal foundations for building

The delicate leaves of a scented geranium, here trained as a standard, are attractive even when not blooming. Long-blooming lobelia spills out at the base of the geranium for a colorful effect.

Blue lobelia with its draping, rounded shape takes on elegance when elevated on a pedestal. A groundcover of spring-blooming columbine provides color throughout summer and into fall.

A container of flowers can be placed in a border for decoration, to add interest and seasonal bloom, or to hide a bare spot.

Casual pedestals of upside-down terra-cotta pots lift formal urns, planted with ivy trained into basket shapes. The planters welcome visitors at the entrance to Ryan Gainey's garden.

Creeping phlox, tucked into pockets of soil at different levels, soften the stone wall's hard edges with pastel colors and rounded mounds of deep green foliage.

rock gardens. It is yet another garden miracle that many plants can grow with only a small space for their roots and minimal requirements for water and nutrients. One gardening friend bought a country property with an ancient, collapsed barn. After hauling the remains of the barn boards away, the new owner couldn't afford the steep price to remove the foundation. He began to experiment with the site, tentativly placing a few plants between the stones. Like a boy in a candy shop, he couldn't stop. Today he is paid the highest compliment. No one notices the stone foundation, but rather, visitors admire the gorgeous garden.

You don't have to inherit a tumble-down farm to enjoy a garden in a rock wall. The ideal way to construct a rock garden in a stone wall is to plant it as you build the wall, adding one layer of soil and plants before positioning the next level of stones. Each pocket of soil should slant down, away from the wall surface, to catch rainwater and to allow the plant stems to grow up and out through the openings between the stones. The best rock-garden plants are small and low growing. Drought-tolerant plants are a good choice, too (see the list of plants for strawberry pots on page 20), as catching rainwater on a near-vertical surface can be a chancy situation.

The spaces between stones or bricks in paths and terraces are also good pockets for plants. Under the stones, the plants' roots are insulated from extreme cold in the winter and intense heat in the summer. The stones slow the evaporation of moisture and protect tender roots from the heavy tread of passersby compressing the soil. I've had good luck with a courtyard planting. The courtyard once had gardens that bordered an unsightly lawn. The grass was cut in ruts from wheelbarrows and bicycles, and killed outright in large spots where construction workers had piled materials. Lawn grass, the most overrated, demanding and unforgiving of plants, is nearly impossible to maintain in this situation. Disgusted, we tore out the lawn and replaced it with large flat stones that could easily support the heavy traffic and occasional equipment. At first the new courtyard looked more like a graveyard than the garden terrace I had envisioned. We persevered, planting creeping and trailing plants and miniature bulbs between the stones.

The hard edges of the paving stones softened as the plants grew, filling the gaps with color and tumbling over the stones. Some uninvited plants—sunflowers, black-eyed Susans and cosmos—seeded themselves, too; we liked their looks, so we left them. I was surprised to learn that many of the plants grew beautifully but as dwarfs because the growth of their roots was curbed by the stone. Their blooming, however, was not at all diminished.

Today, several years later, this courtyard is a favorite place for us to sit or entertain guests. Because of the surrounding stucco walls and the heavy stone floor, the garden is protected from strong winds and holds the heat longer than open spaces. Plants here bloom a week or two earlier than the same, unprotected plants on the other side of the wall, and they stay awhile longer.

A raised bed in the center of this terrace is surrounded by many gardens. The sides of the raised bed are high enough to support tomatoes growing down over the edges. This is easier and more attractive than growing tomatoes in cages or staking them. Red tomatoes are decorative, and off the ground the fruit stays clean and easy to pick.

Spaces between the stones in a courtyard are packed with creeping herbs, tiny bulbs, annuals and perennials, all selected because they are tough plants that will survive if walked on. A few uninvited plants also seeded themselves, including the black-eyed Susan in the foreground. In spite of its height, it was allowed to stay because it broke up the monotony of low-growing plants while remaining attractive, neat and well behaved.

A lattice gazebo is a good place to hang baskets of flowers. In front of the gazebo two raised beds are filled with pots of flowers, creating an outdoor garden room.

At Meadowbrook Farm, geometric beds creatively turn a vegetable garden into a formal, stylized garden. Each square bed is accented with a container.

DESIGNING A CONTAINER AND CONTAINER GARDENS

"In his garden every man may be his own artist without apology or explanation," wrote Louise Beebe Wilder, an extraordinary gardener at the turn of the century. A garden is as personal as a wardrobe. Once you've become acquainted with the rules of good garden design, feel free to disregard any you don't like, as you would a style of clothing.

The principles of design that work for gardens apply to containers and container gardens. A garden is a garden, whether the plants are in containers or in the ground. Many container gardeners find they can redesign groupings easily, relying on castors or wheels added to the bottom of wooden containers, or plant dollies (available in all sizes) to help move the plants around until they achieve a look they like. Containers are a wonderful way to learn about garden design and combinations because you can't make a mistake. If you don't like your first arrangement you change it. The containers are easily moved. One terrace gardener I know plans for changes three times during the garden season. He starts seeds and cuttings in a room with a southern exposure, wheeling them out for display when the plants are a good size, and removing any containers after the plants have finished their bloom.

There are a few basic principles to heed when designing individual containers. Most containers, no matter what size, will be more attractive if something is "spilling" over the edges. The smaller containers are attractive filled with one plant that spills out, but the larger containers need to be thought through. In a large barrel or bushel basket, plant something bushy and upright in the center and surround it with a cascading plant. The contrast of growing habits will make your container look abundant and beautiful.

The plant you want to be the star of the container may be featured in the center. Some plants by virtue of their beauty, and some by virtue of their strangeness, demand attention and set the stage. 'Rosette' impatiens are always scene stealers with their miniature, rose-shaped flowers in prolific bloom all summer. (This is the most popular flowering seed in the

This is one of a pair of urns that light up a shady terrace. The star of this shady container is the 'Rosette' impatiens, the most popular flower seed in the Burpee catalog. Other single-flowered impatiens join with the lime-green-veined leaves of a scented geranium in the foreground and the red tubular flowers of fuchsia. By summer's end the variegated Algerian ivy (Hedera canariensis 'Variegata') runs over the edge and trails like a wedding gown out onto the terrace.

A standard-grown lantana is surrounded by impatiens and heliotrope.

Burpee catalogue and has held that same lofty status for many years.) Caladiums with their large leaves in garish colors are quick to grab attention and very difficult to ignore, but I would never call them beautiful. Each of these is in its own way a star, and each has its place. Other plants are selfless, never drawing attention to themselves but rather quietly enhancing the plants around them. Ivies, in all their variety, do this. Many foliage houseplants are selfless as well. Consider surrounding the center of attention with heart-leaved philodendrons (*Philodendron oxycardium*), plants that don't mind neglect and survive in dim corners, and with their easy manners seem to respond with "I love you" no matter how they are treated. Consider also Swedish ivy (*Plectranthus australis*), with 1- to 2-inch waxy, scalloped leaves, and creeping fig (*Ficus pumila*), with 1-inch heart-shaped leaves. Both grow so thickly they can quickly form a dense carpet to show off a "star."

Blend plants with interesting foliage in containers of flowers. Those with beautiful foliage but few flowers shouldn't be overlooked. Green foliage comes in many different shades and textures; consider the shiny green of peony leaves to the dark green filigree leaves of ferns, the dark green grasslike foliage of liriopes to the quilted and puckered light green to blue-green broad leaves of hostas. Don't forget that green is a color too. Whole containers or container gardens can be designed with different combinations of green foliage texture. There is nothing like a quiet, restful, shady green spot to raise the spirits.

Silvery and variegated foliage, such as that of artemisia and dusty miller, can spotlight favorite flowers. Lamb's ears, like a soft gray cashmere sweater, adds a texture and feel all it's

This nonchalant mixture imitates nature by capturing the casual interweaving of flowers in a wild meadow. It is perfectly at home on the deck of a log cabin where it harmonizes with the surrounding fields.

Morning glories and ivy usually climb upward, but they are equally at home twining together as they clamber down the sides of large containers. Petunias, lantanas and scented geraniums grow up, giving height to the top.

own. Often colorful foliage alone creates an interesting container. The brightly colored, even brassy, foliage of coleus can brighten a shady corner. The soft splashes of pink on dark green leaves make polka-dot plant eye-catching. See also Annuals with Colorful Foliage, page 47.

If the container is to be seen only from the front, mass a background of plants with beau-tiful, lush foliage. The sparsely flowering scented geraniums are a good choice. Upright-growing plants that can reach several feet in height, they are grown mostly for their foliage with its varied and beautiful textures and its fragrance. They are avail-able with leaves of many styles, from crimped, ruffled and curled to deeply cut to broad, velvety, smooth and rough.

The shimmering, silvery leaves of dusty miller encircle Marguerite daisies. Variegated ivy drapes over the side.

COLOR

Color is personal. We are each drawn to different colors because they make us feel good. Some people love a carnival of bright, bold, brassy colors, while oth-ers prefer the subtle romance of soft pastels. Ask yourself whether the location you have in mind for the container is to be used for parties and enter-taining or as a quiet area in which to read a book. Think about the mood you want to create and plan your colors ac-cordingly.

The corner of a small terrace filled with plants can be as warming and cozy as a fireside in winter, or as cool and re-freshing as a pool in summer, depending on the colors used. The hot colors of the sun, yel-low, red and orange, are warm-ing. The cold colors of the sea, blue, purple and white, are cool-ing. The colors chosen should complement the colors of the surroundings; take into account the walls, the furniture, the nearby garden, the floor. Ce-ment, natural wood, slate and other muted backgrounds will not compete with most flower colors and are a quiet back-drop. However, a red flower won't be dazzling against a red brick wall, whereas a bright yellow one would. Discreet use of color can brighten an other-wise dull area.

The container itself shouldn't distract from the planting, and the colors of the planting should harmonize with the color of the container. Both the container and the flowers should comple-ment any furniture or fabrics in the area. Bold colors such as yellow, orange and scarlet show up best in the sunlight. They appear to change throughout the day, depending on the avail-able light, as the sun moves across the sky and peeks in and out from behind clouds, trees and buildings. Subtler col-ors such as white, lavender, vi-olet, pink and blue become washed out and overpowered in direct sunlight and have more impact in the shade.

Green, the most prominent garden color, is the one most overlooked in planning. Shades

Coordinate the colors of the pot and flowers for greater impact. These 'Lemon Gem' marigolds are eye-catching in a blue pot. A watering can is decorative as well as functional sitting among a mixture of pots.

Orange and blue flowers are a happy match, a striking contrast all too infrequent. Here at Wave Hill, each plant—orange tuberous begonia and blue lobelia—has its own pot, and the pots are alternated at the base of a potted tree.

A sunny combination of white geraniums ringed by blue lobelias will bloom together all summer.

of green in foliage vary from deep, dark green, to light, pale green, with gray-green, sea-green and blue-green in between. It is an interesting exercise to see how many shades of green you can discover in your garden. Study how they complement each other, and you will be more aware of how to add dimension to your color design.

The size of the flower as well as the color affects how it will be seen. Using large, more boldly colored flowers, you need fewer to make an impact than with delicate, softer ones. A plant with delicate foliage and tiny blossoms, whatever the color, will lighten and soften the overall effect, whereas a large, solid flower of a bright color would detract from all surrounding flowers.

While the palette of flower colors is almost limitless, it is best to confine the colors used in a single container to one or two (not including green, of course), depending on its size. When selecting for color, remember that colors appear to change according to the colors near them. Bold, neon colors can dwarf or overpower a delicately shaded plant. By the same token, one flower's beauty is often enhanced by its neighbor.

A yellow-foliaged plant would look anemic placed with light green plants, but would be a lovely contrast for a dark green plant. A light yellow flower can make a blue or purple flower more vibrant. One flower can look very different in the same setting but with different neighbors. The intensity of color affects how it relates to the colors next to it. Occasionally prejudiced against the colors of various flowers, I've later admired them when they're grown in another's garden where their beauty is enhanced by the right neighbor.

If you organize color in single-color plantings in numerous easily movable containers, you have at your hands an extremely versatile decorating tool. Your "colors" can be moved easily into different compositions. Note, though, that the crowding of too many colors can lessen an effect from rich to scattered. It is sometimes better to be less lavish. My advice is to enjoy the best part of container gardening: moving the containers around. If two colors clash or detract from each other, one can be moved. Sometimes a distance of only a few feet can make a difference in what clashes and what complements.

FRAGRANCE

Fragrance is the icing on the cake, the finishing touch. In container gardens, which are frequently enjoyed up close, fragrance can be an important component. Don't neglect the influence of fragrance for adding charm to a garden. Bright flowers alone do not make a beautiful garden. A garden is at its best if it is a feast for the senses. Fragrance will be long remembered, perhaps even after the garden is forgotten. Flower fragrances differ enormously, from the deeply intoxicating, heady perfume of gardenias all the way to the unpleasant odor of skunk cabbages. Some fragrances, like the musky, knock-'em-dead punch of paperwhite narcissus, can overpower a room and may be either loved or hated. In between the extremes

are a variety of scents: pine, the lemony scent of verbena, the honey of alyssum, the mint of pennyroyal, the unmistakeable scent of many roses and the vanilla of heliotrope.

Most of the strongly scented flowers are white with thick petals. Some fragrant flowers, such as lavender, hold their fragrance long after the flower has been picked, dried and shriveled, lingering sometimes for years. Such flowers are the main ingredients for potpourri. Perhaps the fact that the fragrance of many flowers lessens during high heat and drought has to do with the diminished plumpness of their petals and a waning of the oils that hold their fragrance. Plants with showy flowers rarely have fragrant leaves. Almost always the fragrance of foliage is re-

Herbs with fragrant foliage are good choices for planting between paving stones. The creeping thyme seen here releases its pungent scent when stepped on.

Left: *A collection of petunias, appreciated for their sweet scent, is combined with pugent-scented lantanas and scented geraniums. Neither the ivy nor the blue salvia has fragrance of its own.* Right: *In each of these half-barrel plantings, fragrant roses trained as standards bloom above geraniums and vincas. They are randomly placed for visitors to enjoy their perfume and beauty.*

freshing, and those who can't bear the heavy, sweet smell of some flowers will find the foliage fragrances, appealing. Pine is probably the best known of the foliage fragrances because it is available in many commercial products, but there are so many others. The scented geranium family has hundreds of different, named hybrids, each with a different fragrance. Their foliage includes apple, lemon, pear, rose, lavender, nutmeg, chocolate, champagne and other fragrances. Scented geraniums have only small, dainty flowers in the spring, so aren't as popular today as their showy cousins, the geraniums with the large bubbles of blooms that never cease throughout the summer. It is said that more than two hundred varieties of scented geranium were available in the early nineteenth century, but today there are so many more that no one seems to be counting.

Some plants send mixed messages of fragrance. The spring starflower (*Ipheion uniflorum*) has mint-scented flowers and onion-scented leaves; what makes them compatible is that the leaves don't release their fragrance unless they are crushed. Frequently fragrant-foliage plants hold their fragrance to themselves unless they are brushed against or touched, and many stingy plants with fragrant foliage can be forced to share their fragrance only when one of their leaves is crushed. (These plants, however, always have a leaf or two to spare.) To avoid disappointment, it is important to know which plants withhold their fragrance and which plants willingly scent the air. Most plants are more fragrant on a hot and humid day, after a rain, or when slapped by a sharp frost. Some moonflowers, for example, release their fragrance only at night.

There are many fragrant flowers from which to choose. The table on the following pages lists just a few in each plant category.

FRAGRANT PLANTS FOR GROWING IN CONTAINERS

Shrubs

COMMON NAME	LATIN NAME	SCENT AND TIME OF BLOOM
Daphne	*Daphne* species	Flowers sweetly floral; spring, some summer and fall
Mock orange	*Philadelphus* species	Flowers are strongly sweet like orange blossoms; spring
Rose	*Rosa* species	Flower scents vary from musk to sweet; summer to fall in the North, year 'round in temperate climates (not all varieties are scented)
Summer sweet*	*Clethra alnifolia*	Flowers have a sweet fragrance; summer
Witch hazel	*Hamamelis* species	Flowers sweetly spiced; winter

Annuals

COMMON NAME	LATIN NAME	SCENT AND TIME OF BLOOM
Flowering tobacco*	*Nicotiana sylvestris*	Flowers are sweetly scented (fragrance is stronger at night); summer
Heliotrope	*Heliotropium arborescens*	Flowers sweetly scented with vanilla; summer in the North, year 'round in temperate climates
Marigold	*Tagetes* species	Flowers and foliage with a pungent spicy fragrance; summer
Nasturtium*	*Tropaeolum* species	Flowers and foliage have a peppery scent; spring, summer and fall
Stock	*Matthiola incana*	Flowers are heavily sweet-scented; summer
Sweet alyssum*	*Lobularia maritima*	Flowers have a honey scent; spring, summer and fall

*Grows in part shade

(continued)

Perennials

COMMON NAME	LATIN NAME	SCENT AND TIME OF BLOOM
Columbine	*Aquilegia vulgaris*	Flowers have haylike scent; spring
Daylily	*Hemerocallis* 'Hyperion'	Flowers have sweet scent; summer (not all cultivars are fragrant)
Funkia	*Hosta* species & hybrids 'Royal Standard' 'Honeybells' 'Sweet Susan'	Flowers have strong sweet scent; summer (not all cultivars are fragrant)
Lavender	*Lavandula angustifolia*	Flowers and foliage are sweet-scented; summer to fall
Peony	*Paeonia* species	Flowers have sweet roselike fragrance; spring (not all cultivars are fragrant)
Pink	*Dianthus* species	Flowers have sweet spicy fragrance; summer
Sweet woodruff	*Galium odoratum*	Flowers have fragrance of new-mown hay; spring
Violet	*Viola* species	Flowers have a sweet floral scent; spring (not all species are fragrant, especially if they have been hybridized)

Vines

COMMON NAME	LATIN NAME	SCENT AND TIME OF BLOOM
Carolina jasmine	*Gelsemium* species	Flowers have sweet floral scent; spring
Hall's honeysuckle	*Lonicera japonica* 'Halliana'	Flowers have strong, sweet fragrance; summer
Star jasmine	*Trachelospermum jasminoides*	Flowers have strong sweet scent; spring, summer
Virgin's bower	*Clematis maximowicziana*	Flowers have sweet floral scent; fall

Bulbs

COMMON NAME	LATIN NAME	SCENT AND TIME OF BLOOM
Crocus	*Crocus chrysanthus*	Flowers have light sweet scent; spring
Crown imperial	*Fritillaria imperialis*	Flowers smell like skunk; spring
Daffodil	*Narcissus* species	Flower fragrance varies with variety, from soft to strong, and musk to sweet; spring

Bulbs (cont.)

COMMON NAME	LATIN NAME	SCENT AND TIME OF BLOOM
Freesia	*Freesia* species	Flowers have strong sweet scent; winter, spring
Hyacinth	*Hyacinthus* species	Flowers have strong sweet scent; spring
Iris	*Iris* species	Flowers of many varieties have sweet scent; spring, summer
Lily	*Lilium* species	Flowers have strong floral scent: summer (not all hybrids are fragrant)
Lily of the valley	*Convallaria majalis*	Flowers have strong, sweet scent; spring
Snowdrop	*Galanthus* species	Flowers have a sweet scent; winter, spring
Spring starflower	*Ipheion uniflorum*	Flowers have sweet minty fragrance, foliage when crushed smells like onion; spring
Tulip	*Tulipa* species	Flowers have sweet floral fragrance; spring (not all cultivars are fragrant)

Herbs

COMMON NAME	LATIN NAME	SCENT AND TIME OF BLOOM
Bee balm	*Monarda* species	Foliage has mint fragrance; summer
Lemon balm	*Melissa officinalis*	Foliage has lemon scent; summer
Mint	*Mentha* species	Foliage has assorted mint fragrance including spearmint and peppermint; spring, summer, fall
Pennyroyal	*Mentha pulegium*	Foliage has minty scent; spring, summer, fall
Pineapple sage	*Salvia elegans*	Foliage has pineapple scent; summer, fall
Scented geranium	*Pelargonium* species	Broad range of foliage fragrance including lemon, rose, apple, cinnamon and wintergreen; spring, summer, fall (winter indoors or frost-free areas)
Wormwood	*Artemisia* species	Foliage has medicinal fragrance; spring, summer, fall

WINNING PLANT COMBINATIONS

The possibilities of plant combinations in containers is endless. While color is the single most important element holding partnerships together, the texture of the foliage and the shape of the mature plant should also be considered. To get you started in selecting your own combinations you might want to try a few of these. The following combinations work especially well together.

Winning Combinations For Containers in Sun

Korean velvet grass (Zoysia tenuifolia) forms a furry collar that is a frilly complement to the flat, bold leaves of the canna lily. The combination is a show-stopper even before the canna blooms. In the background is burgundy fountain grass (Pennisetum setaceum 'Rubrinia').

Top: *Pots combining yellow pansies and white daisies, repeated on each side of the steps, create a bright ribbon of color to lead first the eyes and then the feet up the steps to the house.* Bottom: *The variety of architectural forms and leaf colors in a container of succulents offers a striking change of pace from the flowering annuals more commonly grown in pots.*

*A whimsical combination for an outdoor table combines lettuce, alyssum and dusty miller around the base of myrtle (*Myrtus communis*) trained as a standard. Atlanta designer Ryan Gainey is unconcerned about the classification of plants, treating them as individuals and combining them to beautiful effect.*

*At Wave Hill, Marco Polo Stufano takes cuttings from indoor plants in February to grow on for window-box combinations. Here he combines red fuchsia, ivy, blue lobelia and the yellow bell flowers of monkey flower (*Mimulus aurantiacus*).*

*A halo of silver and gold foliage plants highlights the fragrant blue heliotrope (*Heliotropium arborescens*). Included are silver* Euphorbia myrsinites, *golden licorice plant (*Helichrysum petiolatum 'Limelight'*), the variegated, narrow leaves of the alpine wallflower (*Erysimum linifolium 'Variegatum'*) and the ferny foliage of* Argyranthemum frutescens.

In Atlanta, Georgia, a cone-shaped boxwood topiary is encircled by a ring of variegated ivy.

Fragrant purple heliotrope is mixed with pink petunias. Both are draped and bejeweled with the tiny silver leaves of the tender perennial licorice plant, Helichrysum petiolatum.

Winning Combinations For Containers in Shade

Even without flowers, the variation of color and texture in this pot, combining the pointed leaves of bronze coleus with the filigree green of scented geranium, ensures interest for several seasons.

At Callaway Gardens in Georgia, a brightly planted container lights up a shady wall. This unusual color combination works because the burgundy is so dark (almost black) it recedes into the background and makes peace between the warring pink and orange. The flower shapes, too, are interesting in their contrast. The disks of pink impatiens and plumes of orange celosia peek out between the burgundy curtains of coleus.

The personality of a designer frequently is shown in his or her work. Floral designer J. Barry Ferguson's exuberance, playfulness and love of color are reflected in his unusual combination of two kinds of ivy, variegated and plain, draping over the edges of a container filled with ornamental grass, red-streaked caladiums and bleeding heart vine (Clerodendrum thomsoniae).

In Jackson Hole, Wyoming, a shady corner on the deck of a log cabin is brightened by a whisky barrel of flowers including pink and white wax begonias and impatiens surrounded by the twinkling eyes of lobelia.

A simple but old-fashioned and romantic combination of white, single-flowered, hybrid tuberous begonia, pink, double-flowered Begonia × semperflorens-cultorum *and blue browallia.*

At Bayberry Nursery on Long Island, the charm of a half barrel of polka-dot plant surrounded by dusty miller is hard to resist.

Sprawling, bright orange nasturtiums and bushy blue browallias are planted in matching half barrels at the edge of a shady porch. The overhead hanging basket of browallia highlights what is planted below by using the same plant. This repetition holds the grouping together.

J. Barry Ferguson packs his containers to give a full look. His colorful arrangement for shade includes a fern, mahogany-red wax begonia, Algerian ivy and caladium.

SELECTING THE PLANTS

Some plants make the world better—they give so freely of their blossoms even when neglected or abused, and ask so little in return. Impatiens, geraniums and pansies are like that. At the other extreme are plants that demand constant attention or they will sulk, hang their heads and wilt. It seems their purpose in life is to test our tolerance. (There is only one plant whose commands I jump to obey; like my mother before me, I am addicted to the beauty and fragrance of the gardenia.) Most plants fall somewhere in between the easygoing and the prima donna. It is useful, before purchasing a plant, to know what care is necessary for its maintenance. Theoretically, any plant will grow in a container if the container has soil deep enough for the plant's roots, and the proper conditions of light, heat, water and nutrients are met. "A plant for every place" is the gardener's chant. The trick is to match each plant with the condition it would choose, if it had the ability to do so.

As the earth has seemingly shrunk at an incredible rate, plants from all over the globe have reached America. Their diverse and even exotic origins are represented in gardens that make no pretense of growing any but the most common plants. Few of us take the time to think about where our favorite plants come from, but doing so can be helpful in understanding the needs of each plant. Many of our most popular plants we take for granted, not recognizing the distances they have traveled and the adjustments they have made to very different living conditions. Impatiens from the humid jungles of Africa have adapted to conditions all across America. Bleeding heart from Japan, herbs from the Mediterranean, bougainvillea from South America, and potatoes from the mountains of Peru are just a few of our most popular plants. Amazing is the variety of situations from which different plants come to us, yet they flourish together almost side by side. A bulb garden alone is as varied in origins as a United Nations assembly, with fancy-leaved caladiums from the riverbanks of the Amazon, blackberry lilies from China, spring beauty from Argentina, gladiolus from South Africa, foxtail lilies from the Himalayan Mountains, dahlias from Mexico, crocuses from Southern Europe and glory-of-the-snows from the mountains of Asia Minor. Do plants from such disparate parts of the world qualify for a summit meeting in the garden?

The tulip family has ancestors from Central Asia, Italy, North Africa, Crete, Great Britain and Persia. Sometimes plants proudly announce their origin in their Latin names. *Tulipa persica*, for example, is from Persia. Don't be misled by a plant's common name, though, because it can be deceiving. The popular houseplant Swedish ivy is really from Australia; its common name honors the country that first brought it indoors.

Raising a large urn onto a pedestal adds formality and importance, making the urn a focal point. The rounded, upright shape of the Marguerite daisies is emphasized in contrast to the assortment of ivies trailing downward.

You can refer to *Hortus*, third edition, to learn about where plants originated. Once the plant's origins are known, it is easier to cater to its preferences. In the case of a plant from the high Andes, it could take some doing to make it feel at home in the low-altitude plains of the Midwest, but if it is from a tropical jungle climate, it can be tricked more easily, surrounded by the warm humid air summer provides for most of this country. Knowing your plants and their needs will help you avoid disappointment. Many a plant is doomed to failure because the gardener doesn't take the time to get to know its needs. Don't select a plant and put it in a no-win situation. Wax begonias from South and Central America, for example, prefer partial shade. If grown in full sun they look like they are in great pain; sunburned, scorched, dehydrated, and garish as their leaves turn a burnt red. Grown in part shade, their leaves are plump, pert and dark green, with open, lively and bright flowers.

Before you select the plants for your containers, note the movement of the sun over the area where you will be growing. Most plants considered sun-lovers require six to eight hours of sun a day. Other plants will perform with an afternoon or a morning of sun. It is important to provide the direct sunlight a plant needs.

WHERE TO START

It's always fun to grow an unusual plant, or to try one with a reputation for being difficult, but first look for pleasing combinations of the plants you know or are comfortable growing. Some flowers and combinations are overused. But even though some plants may be considered "common," remember that each plant is an individual and will grow a little differently from its sister, especially when placed in a different container, grouped with different plants and viewed in a different setting. Combine both common and new plants with imagination and creativity, and you'll see familiar flowers in new ways. Sprinkle old plant friends with whimsy and you'll have the pleasure of a new creation. Some of your creations may not be all you'd hoped for, but many will show their beauty and prove to be obliging, undemanding friends. Gardening, whether in containers or out in a yard, is like that. It opens up a whole world of exciting possibilities and dreams.

The principles of planting containers and combining them are simple, but the greater the number of containers involved in a grouping, the more complex the process becomes. Large containers will shade smaller ones if they are placed side by side. Use this to advantage and set those plants that are shade-lovers below the sun-seekers. Impatiens, shaded by a ficus tree, will show their appreciation by dressing the ficus' bare bottom with colorful blooms. A container garden is a place to have it all.

The plant's shape when full grown should be considered. A hanging basket looks best with a plant whose habit resembles a fountain rather than a rocket. Standing pots are more flexible. They can resemble ice cream cones with rounded tops, rocket ships heading skyward, lollipops on long stems or barbells with a ball in the air.

If you are combining more than one type of plant in a container, make sure they won't fight. Plants need good neighbors, and this is more important in containers than out in the garden. Some vines are ruthlessly ambitious and will climb over anything, suffocating it in the process. Some plants, mint for example, have roots that travel in speeds in excess of ninety miles an hour, ramming any plant in their path. (I grow mint by itself where, alone in its container, it is constricted into good behavior.) Which plants make good companions is learned mostly through trial and error. Whenever you notice one plant overwhelming another is the time to transplant or restrain the offending plant. I have a favorite combination for a shady terrace of white impatiens surrounded by trailing blue lobelia. The first year the impatiens bullied and crowded the lobelia until it receded and died. The second year I bought a plastic pot of impatiens and planted them, pot and all, in the center of a larger container. That kept them in their place, and the lobelia twinkled happily over the rim of the pot and down its sides. This illustrates a useful way to "contain" any aggressive plant within a container.

When a plant is difficult or if you're unsure of its reputation, it is simpler to place it alone or with others of its species in a container until you understand its behavior. Single planting containers can then be grouped to achieve the combinations you want. Single plantings can have other advantages, too. There are many plants that give a minimum of five months of bloom in warm weather, and are so handsome that they look well planted alone; impatiens, geraniums and tuberous begonias are among these.

How do you select from annuals, perennials, bulbs, herbs, vegetables, shrubs, houseplants and vines for your containers? While each classification has its advantages (as well as disadvantages), the classifications themselves are rather arbitrary. Many plants fall into more than one classification. Ivy, for example, is variously considered a groundcover, houseplant and vine. Various species of begonia are considered bulbs, houseplants and annuals. This is a situation where classification isn't worth a worry. Each plant should be selected on its merits and on your needs. Mother Nature doesn't segregate plants and neither should we. Mix and match plants from all classifications for a diverse, long-blooming garden of containers. Make an educated decision when selecting a plant, though, and get acquainted with the extraordinary diversity within any classification.

Many a time I've dismissed a plant as not being worth growing only to see it grown beautifully by someone else. Gardening is not an exact science. The many variables are not always obvious, so if you are not satisfied the first time you grow a plant, give it a second chance.

A brief discussion of plant classifications and recommended plants follows. The plant portrait sections in other *Burpee American Gardening Series* books (*Annuals, Perennials, Flowering Shrubs, Vegetables, Groundcovers, Shade Gardening, Bulbs* and *Herbs*) will provide detailed descriptions of specific plants and will help you choose wisely, with an understanding of each plant's needs.

Annuals

Annuals are those plants that bloom the first season from seeds sown in spring. They give many months of continuous bloom before going to seed or being killed by heavy frost and winter weather. Most annuals have quick growth, shallow roots, long bloom time, a wide assortment of colors and require relatively easy care. All of this makes them a natural choice for growing in containers. Any annual can be grown in a container, but some—asters, baby's breath and sweet peas, for example—have short blooming periods of a few weeks, and this can be disappointing if you expected them to bloom all summer.

Annuals are divided into three categories: hardy, half-hardy

and tender. The way a seed or young plant is handled will vary according to the category to which it belongs. Hardy annuals are those whose seedlings are able to survive freezing weather. They can be sown in the fall or early spring in permament outdoor containers as soon as the soil can be worked.

In the tradition of "good fences make good neighbors," impatiens are planted inside a plastic pot before they are placed in this concrete urn, to keep their roots from overrunning the roots of the lobelia. This is a bright combination for a shady spot. The white flowers of the impatiens glow in the shadows and reflect the light from a nearby porch in the evening. The delicate trailing foliage and flowers of lobelia rightly complement the larger, flat buttons of impatiens.

Top: *A double impatiens with a variegated leaf is spectacular enough to stand alone in a shady corner. Bottom: Zinnias, flowering all summer, are colorful plants for an entrance. Sweet alyssum has been seeded between the stones at the feet of the container to release fragrance for all who walk by.*

Blue and white is always a winning combination. The large, white leaves of the caladium highlight the blue browallia and double-flowered tuberous begonia.

The variegated, golden leaves of a wax begonia bring light to a shady spot.

LONG-BLOOMING ANNUALS FOR CONTAINERS
(THREE OR MORE MONTHS OF BLOOM)

COMMON NAME	LATIN NAME
Blue daisy	*Felicia amelloides*
Browallia	*Browallia* species**
Busy Lizzy or patient plant	*Impatiens wallerana***
Common heliotrope	*Heliotropium arborescens**
Cupflower	*Nierembergia* species
Dahlia	*Dahlia* species
Flossflower	*Ageratum* species
Flowering maple	*Abutilon* species**
Flowering tobacco	*Nicotiana* species**
Forget-me-not	*Myosotis sylvatica***
Four-o'clock	*Mirabilis jalapa*
Geranium	*Pelargonium* species
Lobelia	*Lobelia erinus***
Marigold	*Tagetes* species
Monkey flower	*Mimulus* species**
Moss rose or sun rose	*Portulaca grandiflora*
Nasturtium	*Tropaeolum* species**
'New Guinea' impatiens	*Impatiens* 'New Guinea'**
Pansy	*Viola* × *wittrockiana***
Periwinkle or vinca	*Catharanthus roseus*
Petunia	*Petunia* species*
Pot marigold	*Calendula officinalis*
Sage	*Salvia* species*
Snapdragon	*Antirrhinum* species
Stock	*Matthiola incana**
Swan River daisy	*Brachycome iberidifolia*
Sweet alyssum	*Lobularia maritima***
Tuberous begonia	*Begonia* × *tuberhydrida***
Verbena	*Verbena* species*
Wax begonia	*Begonia* × *semperflorens***
Wishbone flower	*Torenia* species**
Zinnia	*Zinnia* species

*Some species are fragrant
**Grows in part shade

Most hardy annuals don't tolerate strong heat, and therefore bloom in early spring and continue until killed by hot summer weather. Forget-me-nots (*Myosotis sylvatica*), pansies and sweet peas are hardy annuals. Alyssum is also hardy but it is an exception, blooming spring, summer and fall, and even self-sowing to bloom the following year. It is compatible with most plants and a good choice to seed over bulbs, at the base of a rosebush or other flowering shrub, and to edge a pot of perennials. (It is an excellent choice for crevices, edging, strawberry pots and any place that a fluff of dainty white flowers and the

ANNUALS WITH COLORFUL FOLIAGE

COMMON NAME	LATIN NAME	FOLIAGE COLOR
Beefsteak plant	*Perilla frutescens*	Burgundy
Dusty miller	*Cineraria maritima*	Silver
Foliage plant, coleus	*Coleus* species	Multicolor or bicolor foliage, including white, green, pink, red, brown, orange.
Polka-dot plant	*Hypoestes* species	Bicolor foliage: pink, green, white or burgundy

*Another variation of the blue and white color scheme for a sunny planting and providing long summer bloom is the perennial Viola 'Princess Blue' and the zinnia 'Star White' (*Zinnia angustifolia*).*

sweet aroma of honey is welcome. One of the easiest annuals to grow, sweet alyssum blooms from seed in approximately 40 to 60 days, depending on the weather.)

In the spring, after all danger of frost is past, half-hardy annuals are sown. Once established, they can survive light frost in the fall, but a heavy frost or prolonged cold spell will see their demise. Examples include the flowering maple and polka-dot plant, half-hardy annuals adaptable to life as houseplants in the winter. The flowering maple, with leaves the shape of those of the maple tree, has nodding, bell-shaped flowers in yellow, orange, red or white. If treated well, it will repay the gardener with flowers year 'round. The polka-dot plant is not grown for its flowers but for its dark green foliage, which appears to be splashed with paint; the varieties 'Pink Splash', 'White Splash', 'Confetti', and 'Wine Red' salute its colorful variations.

Tender annuals are the most fragile and can be planted only in warm soil. They won't survive even a light frost. Begonias, impatiens and lantanas are tender annuals. Begonias, geraniums and lantanas can be grown through the fall as houseplants, given a rest (see page 79), and returned outdoors the following spring.

The most frequently "seen about town" annuals include impatiens, geraniums and petunias. All are well-behaved and accommodating, but many other annuals will please you as easily. Above, and at left, is a list of easy-care annuals ideal with which to start.

Perennials

A perennial, strictly speaking, is any plant that survives more than two winters, but I will use the word to mean such herbaceous plants as daylilies, chrysanthemums and hostas that are grown for their ornamental

Campanula porcharskyana is a long-blooming, easy-care perennial that twinkles wherever it lives. It is equally at home in a partially sunny window box, between paving stones and bordering a perennial garden.

A single planter with brightly colored zinnia, pink lisianthus and white sweet alyssum decorates a dock at Mohonk Mountain House.

flowers and foliage. The stems of herbaceous perennials (with a few exceptions) die back to the ground each winter, but their strong, hardy roots send up new shoots each spring, usually for many years. The best results with most perennials come after the second year, a time when many perennials first come into bloom. As with all classifications, there are exceptions, and *Coreopsis* 'Early Sunrise'ᵛᵖ and *Viola* 'Princess Blue' are two; both bloom approximately 80 days after sowing and stay in bloom for months. Most perennials bloom for just a few weeks or a month, but some are long-bloomers. *Aster* × *frikartii* 'Wonder of Staffa', bellflower (*Campanula carpatica*), balloon-flower (*Platycodon grandiflorus*), catmint (*Nepeta* species), lavender (*Lavandula*) and daylily (*Hemerocallis* 'Stella de Oro') will bloom for three months or longer

and return to bloom summer after summer. The Princess series of perennial violets (*Viola cornuta*) blooms in early spring, even through light frost, into early summer, then slows its bloom in the heat of summer and is rejuvenated in the fall.

While their flowers may last only a few weeks, many perennials have decorative foliage that is attractive for months. The drama of foliage shouldn't be overlooked and should be planned for as carefully as for bloom. Consider the silvery, woolly leaf of lamb's ears, the silvery, lacy foliage of artemisia and the flat, bold burgundy leaves of *Heuchera* 'Palace Purple'. Hosta, grown primarily for foliage, includes specimens with frosty blue leaves (*Hosta* 'Krossa Regal'), dark green leaves with golden borders (*Hosta Fortunei* 'Aureo-marginata'), light green leaves that turn to gold for the summer (*Hosta* 'Gold Standard'), sage-green leaves with sparkling white edges and a bluish cast to the undersides (*Hosta undulata* 'Albo-marginata') or lance-shaped, yellow-green leaves with contrasting deep green edges (*Hosta* 'Kabitan'). My favorite is the rather plain, green heart-shaped leaves of *Hosta* 'Royal Standard'. It is rarely noticed by the casual visitor until summer's end, when 2-foot stalks of white trumpet flowers appear with a sweet fragrance that generously scents the air; if you are within a few yards of a clump of 'Royal Standard', you'll be pleasantly intoxicated by its sweet fragrance. The hosta family is extensive, and this is only a small sampling of the great variety.

Ferns with their narrow foliage lend a light and airy effect to a container planting. The Japanese painted fern (*Athyrium niponicum pictum*) is one of the most decorative, with wine-red midribs and metallic gray-green leaves softening to white. Lady fern (*Athyrium Filix-femina*) has feathery, bright green fronds with deeply cut leaves and the Christmas fern (*Polystichum acrostichoides*) has long, narrow, dark green fronds and leaflets that are often twisted. Christmas ferns are one of the most cold-hardy ferns and often the first to appear in spring with silvery fiddleheads. There are many more ferns from which to choose, and they are all good choices for shady containers as long as they receive the deep, highly organic soil they require along with plenty of moisture. Even the asparagus fern (*Asparagus setaceus*), usually categorized as a houseplant, is an undemanding and attractive plant for outdoor containers.

The new popularity of perennial ornamental grasses is sweeping the country. Imaginative designers are adding them to containers for the beauty of their textures and their graceful movement as they dance in the gentlest breezes. They are particularly dramatic in autumn, when their colors change and many of them flower. There is a wide choice of colors and heights. Fountain grass (*Pennisetum orientale*) has gray-green foliage 30 inches high, and many small cottony pink flowers that clothe long stems. Japanese blood grass (*Imperata cylindrica*) is shorter, with 2-

FLOWERS RECOMMENDED FOR OUTDOOR CONTAINERS

NOTE: *Most need at least 6 hours of sunshine per day. Begonia, caladium, coleus and impatiens will grow in shade.*

FLOWER	VARIETY	MINIMUM CONTAINER SIZE—WIDTH & DEPTH (1 plant per container unless noted)
AGERATUM	Blue Ball	6 in.
	Blue Chip Hybrid	6 in.
BEGONIA†	Most varieties	6 in.
CELOSIA	Floradale® and others, especially dwarf	6 in.
COLEUS†	Rainbow, Mixed Colors	6 in.
GERANIUM*	Colorcade and others	8 in.
GOURDS	Small Fancy Mixed Varieties	12 in. (3 plants on trellis)
IMPATIENS†	Glitters and others	6 in.
LOBELIA†	Sapphire	6 in.
MARIGOLD, American	Burpee's Climax Hybrids	8 in.
	Burpee's Lady Hybrids	8 in.
MARIGOLD, dwarf French	Goldie and others	6 in.
MARIGOLD, mule	Burpee's Nuggets™†	6 in.
	Red and Gold Hybrid	6 in.
MOONFLOWER	————	12 in. (3–4 plants on trellis)
MORNING GLORY	Heavenly Blue and others	12 in. (3–4 plants on trellis)
NASTURTIUM	Fordhook® Favorites†	12 in. (3–4 plants on trellis or trailing)
	Jewel, Mixed Colors	6 in.
PANSY*	Imperial Blue and others	6 in. (2 plants)
PETUNIA†	Royalty and others	8 in.
PHLOX	Twinkle and others	6 in.
PORTULACA†	Magic Carpet® and others	6 in.
SALVIA	St. John's Fire	6 in.
SWEET ALYSSUM†	Carpet of Snow	6 in.
	Royal Carpet	6 in.
SWEET PEA*	Bijou	6 in.; or 12 in. (4 plants)
ZINNIA	Thumbelina	6 in.

*These varieties stand light frost; all others cannot tolerate frost.
†Good for hanging baskets.

foot foliage, but it draws attention with its remarkable coloring; early in the season the leaves are green at the base, shading into brilliant red, and in fall the entire plant turns flaming scarlet. It tolerates part shade, and I've grown it with success in a woodland garden.

If it's a powder blue color you need for your color scheme, grow blue fescue 'Azurit' (*Festuca* 'Azurit'). With its low (12 inches) height and tufted growth, it reminds one of the hair of a punk rocker—proving once again that Mother Nature has a plant for everyone. The narrow, var-

iegated maiden grass (*Miscanthus sinensis*) makes a dramatic and grateful accent, with 5 feet of fine-textured, silvery green leaves enhanced by crisp narrow bands of white along the edges.

Most perennial plants with attractive foliage can be a fit-

Irises and pansies bloom together for late-spring color. Later the pansies are replaced with such summer annuals as geraniums.

ting backdrop that enhances a favorite flowering plant. Some of the most beautiful plantings consist of a single specimen or type as the central feature with others surrounding it to enhance its beauty.

In northern climates above Zone 6, few perennials grown in containers survive if left outdoors without protection, even though they are hardy in the garden to Zone 3. A general rule is if the temperature of the soil container drops below 20°F, the perennial can't survive. Perennial roots are more protected when planted in the ground, where low temperatures can't reach them as easily. Dr. Allan Armitage, an expert on perennial plants, explains that when he lived in Montreal, Canada, he grew perennial plants in easily movable containers, and once they became dormant from the first prolonged cold, he buried the containers at the bottom of his compost pile for the winter. With several feet of leaves on top they were insulated from the harsh winter weather.

Bulbs

"Bulb" is loosely used by gardeners and horticulturists alike, to refer to those plants that grow from bulblike structures that are harvested, stored, shipped and sold while dormant. The term has come to include everything from true bulbs to corms, rhizomes and tubers, which are easy to confuse because, in the garden, they behave similarly. Regardless of the classification, the most important thing to remember is that these various bulbous structures are all underground food storehouses. Each of the four types of plant is herbaceous, dying down in winter, leaving no permanent stem above ground. Thin, threadlike feeding roots grow out from the bottom of the "bulb" to anchor it in the soil and to take in water and nutrition, but the bulb's real energy is manufactured above ground. If an overzealous gardener, anxious to clean up a bed, removes the dying leaves too early, the bulb will have a diminished bloom the following season or die, depending on how early the foliage has been removed. Their foliage must be allowed to yellow and die, for this is the time when the foliage assists the underground storehouse in replenishing the food supply.

In the case of a container, it may not be important that the bulbs return the following year. In fact, many hardy spring bulbs, if forced to bloom earlier than their normal season, will not recover and bloom again. The sizes of bulbs range from the tiny "fingertip" to a boxer's fist. No matter the size of the package, bulbs are all powerhouses of bloom. The size you see when you purchase bulbs is the space they need underground to grow.

These are plants that love companions and are improved by the company they keep. Unless you are packing many together into a pot to be discarded after bloom, they will behave very well when planted under and around annuals and perennials. Bulbs are tough, solid packages that won't be disturbed by the roots of other plants growing around and under them, as long as you, the gardener, provide enough nutrition by fertilizing as regularly as you water.

Even some summer-blooming bulbs that aren't full figured like lilies, canna lilies, gladiolus and irises grow up leaving bare stems with few leaves near the soil. All of them look better when combined with another plant that will hide the soil. The fragrant hybrid lilies can be planted to grow up through other plants and blossom over their heads. They add fragrance, height and beauty to a pot of annual flowers. Many other summer bulbs fill a pot alone or combine well with other flowers as they grow bushy and full, blooming all summer, and sometimes longer. Among these bulbs are tuberous begonias, dahlias, caladiums and the often overlooked achimenes.

Tuberous begonias are popular for their radiant color and long bloom from early summer until frost. If the bulbs are started indoors in March or the plants are moved indoors before frost, the bloom will be even longer. There are upright and pendulous varieties, with single or double blooms. The Pacific giant hybrid's flowers are ruffled and fully double, up to 6 inches across, with colors that range from yellow, scarlet, apricot and pink to yellow edged with red or white with pink. The 'Crispa Marginata' series are unique bicolor begonias with single large frilled petals, accented with a contrasting edge. Flowers resembling roses dangle from fully branched and drooping stems of the 'Giant Double' hybrid series. The leaves on hanging tuberous begonia (*Begonia* × *tuberhybrida* 'Pendula') can be heart shaped or arrow shaped with plain or serrated edges. The stems are 2 to 4 feet long

Lily bulbs planted close together can be left in a pot from year to year if they are protected from prolonged freezing in the winter.

A mixture of calla lilies will be happy blooming indoors in winter or outdoors in summer, as long as their soil is kept moist and they are given a rest for part of the year.

Hybrid tuberous begonias in this 'Hanging Basket Mix' have been bred with a more fully branched, pendulous habit so they arch down over the rim of their pots.

The quality and intensity of light in a garden is constantly changing. White flowers hold the light and glow in shade as well as twilight. The white tulips in pots and repeated in the terrace garden reflect the dappled sunlight and complement the surrounding evergreen foliage.

VEGETABLES RECOMMENDED FOR OUTDOOR CONTAINERS

NOTE: *Most need at least 6 hours of sunshine per day. The following may do well with less sunlight: Swiss chard, Burpee's 'Curlycress'™, lettuce, parsley and spinach.*

VEGETABLE	VARIETY	MINIMUM CONTAINER SIZE—WIDTH & DEPTH (1 plant per container unless noted)
BEAN, bush snap	Burpee's Greensleeves^{VP}	6 in. (2 each), 12 in. (4 each)
BEAN, pole snap	Kentucky Wonder	12 in. (2–4 plants on poles or trellis)
BEAN, pole lima	King of the Garden	12 in. (2–4 plants on poles or trellis)
CRESS	Burpee's Curlycress™	6 in. (broadcast seed)
CUCUMBER	Burpee Hybrid	12 in. (3 plants on trellis)
	Burpless Hybrid	12 in. (3 plants on trellis)
EGGPLANT	Burpee's Black Beauty	12 in.
	Burpee Hybrid	12 in.
HERBS	Chives*	6 in.
	Oregano*	6 in.
	Sweet Basil	6 in.
	Sweet Marjoram	6 in.
LETTUCE*	Burpee Bibb	6 in.
	Green Ice^{VP}†	6 in.
	Oak Leaf†	6 in.
PARSLEY*†	Extra Curled Dwarf	6 in.
SPINACH*†	Malabar	8 in. (2–3 plants trailing or on trellis)
SUMMER	Burpee Golden Zucchini^{VP}	12 in.
SQUASH	Burpee Hybrid Zucchini	12 in.
STRAWBERRY†	Baron Solemacher	6 in.
SWEET PEPPER	California Wonder	12 in.
	Sweet Banana	12 in.
SWISS CHARD*	Burpee's Fordhook® Giant	6 in.
	Burpee's Rhubarb	6 in.
TOMATO	Burpee's Pixie Hybrid†	8 in. (staked)
	Burpee's Big Girl® Hybrid VF	12 in. (on support)
	Burpee's VF Hybrid	12 in. (on support)
	Basket Pak†	12 in. (on support)
	Red Cherry†	12 in. (on support)
	Yellow Plum†	12 in. (on support)

*These varieties stand light frost; all others cannot tolerate frost.
†Good for hanging baskets.
^{VP}Unauthorized propagation prohibited—U.S. Variety Protection applied for—U.S. Protected Variety

and spill gracefully over the sides of containers, displaying single or double flowers that bloom continuously over the long summer season of southern gardens.

The showy dahlias have a range of sizes, colors and flower shapes. The size of mature plants can be from 1 to 4 feet tall and sometimes more. The colors include everything but blue, with many bicolors. The flower shapes mimic a variety of other flowers including cactus, pompon chrysanthemum and waterlily, in single and double forms.

Bold, brassy caladiums have gorgeous heart-shaped leaves in a kaleidoscope of colors for shade. The only caladiums that come close to being subtle are ones with green ribs and veins on white leaves such as 'Candidum'. 'Fannie Munson' has intense pink leaves with scarlet ribs and a green, splash-painted border. 'Red Flash' is just that, striking red leaves with pink splashes and a green edge. There are many caladium varieties available, all with variations on the same bold patterns, and you'll find their appearance is more subdued when combined with ferns, hostas and other, quieter plants.

And don't forget the achimenes. They are versatile, easy to grow and undemanding. As if that weren't enough, they thrive in shade or semishade, blooming nonstop for many months in the summer. The cascading varieties like 'Fairy Pink', 'Rosy Red' and 'Violet Night' are well suited for hanging baskets, strawberry pots and window boxes.

Herbs and Vegetables

Herbs and vegetables are decorative and often fragrant as well as useful. The deep green curled leaves of parsley or the deep purple, ruffled leaves of purple basil garnish a planter as well as a plate. Brilliant red Swiss chard leaves lend a bright backdrop for flowers, and chard is so productive it can be continuously picked for dinners. Fennel and dill both have soft, fernlike foliage that complements bolder, larger-leafed plants. Most dill fades quickly after bloom and needs to be replanted, but Burpee's dwarf 'Fernland'ᵛᴾ dill is slower to go to seed and will last longer. The foliage of fennel is decorative all summer. Different varieties of scented geraniums have foliage that varies from furry to prickly, curled to flat, lacy to bold, and, in addition, are pleasingly fragrant.

Ornamental pepper 'Candlelight' is an unusual choice for a wall-hanging basket. It blooms in late summer and is a decorative fall plant to move indoors when frost threatens.

Growing herbs and vegetables, even tomatoes, peppers or eggplants, in large pots or tubs is not much different than growing them in a garden. The advantage of disease-free soil is especially important to vegetables susceptible to soil-borne diseases, those that ought to be crop rotated yearly in the garden. The basic gardening principles to remember here are that the pots be deep enough (most vegetables need at least 8 inches for their roots); the plants receive 6 to 8 hours of direct sun daily; that a strong pole or trellis be provided for support when needed. A trellis is sturdier if it is nailed to the inside of a wooden box to give it extra strength for holding the heavier vegetables; the weight of the planting will stabilize the trellis. Stick the planting stakes in the pot and nail them to the container before adding soil or grow the pot next to a wall with a trellis, netting or lattice attached. Peas, beans and other vine crops are very decorative and good candidates for growing against a house or garage. Of course, there's no reason why they have to grow up; they can be attractive growing down the sides of a large container and trailing onto a terrace or porch. Note that many vegetables such as tomatoes and watermelon hold water in their fruit and need more watering than other container plants.

A bushel basket, or any basket, lined with plastic (a garbage bag is fine) and filled with sterile potting soil is a good place to start. Even a plastic bag of potting soil purchased at a nursery and placed whole in the basket will work. Slit holes in the bottom of the bag for drainage to prevent damage from overwatering. If using a plastic bag of potting soil, slash Xs in the top where each individual seed or seedling is to grow. The corners of the plastic are held back so the seedling can be planted. The plastic acts as a mulch to hold the moisture in the soil, prevent weed seed from sprouting, and keep the soil at an even temperature.

Drought-tolerant culinary herbs are at home in a strawberry pot. If placed near the kitchen door they can easily be picked and used as needed.

Fit the plant (or plants) to the pot. Peppers, cucumbers, cantaloupe, tomatoes, squash and watermelon grow roots to a depth of 12 or more inches; the roots of celery, lettuce, and greens grow to 8 inches; spinach, rhubarb, onions, beans, peas, beets and Swiss chard will be somewhere in between. This means that you can't plant a tomato seedling or tomato seeds in an 8-inch-deep pot. Nor should you waste a 12-inch deep pot on a 4- to 6-inch radish root.

Hybrid vegetables are a good choice for container growing. Hybrid seeds are produced by crossing different parents and will grow only one generation of plants. (The offspring from a hybrid may revert to resemble one parent and so lose its superior qualities, so saving seed

from a hybrid is not recommended.) All hybrids are so noted on seed packs, with "hybrid" as part of the seed name. In the case of fruits and vegetables, hybrids are bred primarily for better flavor, but there are lots of other advantages. Most hybrids are heavy yielders that produce more than the older varieties, so the home gardener can enjoy more produce from less growing space. Space-saving plants, the dwarf varieties, mean that a heavily producing plant can fit in a container garden and bring a larger harvest from modest space. Disease resistance is another advantage of hybrids. Look for the letters, V, F or N after variety names where they are printed in catalogs and on seed packs. They indicate that the variety is resistant to verticillum wilt, fursarium wilt or nematodes, respectively. Concern for the environment has encouraged breeding for disease resistance, bringing good results without the use of harmful chemicals.

Dwarf varieties of vegetables are tailor-made for containers because they have smaller roots, suffer less wind damage and are less voracious eaters. Burpee plant breeders, among others, have developed a talented group of dwarf gourmet vegetables as well as miniature or "baby" vegetables ideal for growing in the restricted area of a container. In metropolitan areas, commercial growers supply baby vegetables to fresh-produce markets where they command a high price, fair because it compensates the grower for the extra labor required to pick them.

Baby vegetables tend to be

milder and more tender than their fully grown sisters. As a container gardener, you can pick and serve some of the vegetables you grow as baby vegetables and allow others, in the same crop, to mature to full size. Pick okra young, and pick any summer squash within 24 hours of flowering. Zucchini should be no more than 4 inches long. Even delicious "new" potatoes fit into this category of early-picked vegetables. When selecting vegetables to harvest as "babies," choose only recommended varieties. Some vegetables, when picked early, lack the vitamins, sweetness and flavor that develop only as the vegetables mature. Fortunately there are some baby vegetables, bred for their small size, we heartily recommend. When mature, they provide all the nutrition and flavor their bigger cousins do.

The following is a list of baby vegetables and those vegetables that can be picked while immature. All are mild, tender and full of vitamins, sweetness and flavor.

Beet
 'Burpee Golden'
 'Little Ball'
Carrot
 'Little Finger'
 'Short and Sweet'
 'Thumbelina'
Cucumber
 'Burpee Pickler'
Eggplant
 'Millionaire'
Kolhrabi
 'Grand Duke'
Lettuce
 'Burpee Bibb'
 Romaine, 'Little Gem'

Okra
  'Annie Oakley Hybrid'
  'Clemson Spineless'
Onion
  'Crystal Wax Pickling PBR'ᵛᵖ
Pea
  'Snowbird'
Pumpkin
  'Jack Be Little'
Radish
  'Burpee White'
  'Cherry Belle'
Summer squash
  'Burpee Golden Zucchini'
  'Burpee Hybrid Zucchini'
  'Pic-N-Pic Hybrid'
  'Richgreen Hybrid Zucchini'
  'Sunburst Hybrid'
Tomato
  'Gardener's Delight'
  'Pixie Hybrid II'
  'Sundrop'
  'Sweet 100'
  'Yellow Pear'
Turnip
  'Purple-Top'
  'Tokyo Cross'
  'White Globe'

Succulents

Sedums and sempervivums have an otherworldly appearance and can require some getting use to. They are unabashedly strange, a little like no-neck monsters. However, they have many endearing qualities and are trouble free and easy to grow when given full sun and quick-draining soil. Their plump bodies store water to help them withstand drought. If they are given too much water, they rot or grow in strange shapes. Rarely are they affected by disease.

Their Latin names are descriptive. Sedum is from the Latin *sedeo*, which means "to sit,"

A recycled window box grows an assortment of lettuce, parsley and leeks under a single tomato plant ('Pixie Hybrid II').

A lemon-scented geranium (Pelargonium crispum 'Prince Rupert') is pruned into a column with rosemary growing at its base.

Brussels sprouts are harvested in approximately 95 days from sowing the seed. They are extremely cold-hardy—in fact, the flavor is improved by a few frosts. Even in northern climates they can be grown easily in a deep pot on a sunny terrace.

Culinary herbs can be grown in a portable wooden tray, easy to bring indoors when frost threatens.

A silvery succulent performs well in this blue-and-white metal pot because metal tends to hold the heat, and succulents are heat lovers.

and the plants seem to do just that, whether on walls, cliffs or between rocks. Sempervivum comes from the Latin *semper*, which means "always," and *vivus*, which means "alive." And that's almost how the plant is. I don't want to mislead you into thinking they can withstand any conditions, but they are tough little plants that tolerate diverse situations. They are prolific at sending out shoots with baby plants, hence one common name, hen and chicks. The chicks can be broken off any time of year to start their own families. I simply break off a baby and set it in another crack in my stone wall, where the bottom of the cutting touches soil. I take advantage of its good nature and don't even bother to water the new baby in. More often than not, they grow, sprouting new chicks of their own.

Grown in stone walls or outdoor containers, sempervivums coloration will reflect the seasons. As fall's chilly winds arrive in northern gardens, the edges of sempervivum petals are outlined in red. By winter they have taken on a burgundy glow, and in spring the green starts to reappear. Dull, dirty rose flowers bloom in clusters at the end of 8-inch-long stems in the summer, each daisylike flower about 1 inch across.

Small pots of succulents are decorative as outdoor table centerpieces. Succulents are drought tolerant and can withstand the drying effect of the sun without needing to be watered daily.

RECOMMENDED VARIETIES OF SEDUM AND SEMPERVIVUM

COMMON NAME	LATIN NAME
Burro's tail	*Sedum morganianum*
Hen and chicks, or	
common houseleek	*Sempervivum tectorum*
Stonecrop	*Sedum craigii*
	S. humifusum
	S. lineare variegatum
	S. nevii
	S. rubrotinctum
	S. sieboldii

Dwarf boxwood, clipped and shaped like a bow tie, sports a knot of variegated euonymus.

The tall, long-blooming sedum 'Autumn Joy' in the center of this half barrel changes color with the seasons. In early summer its light green flowers gradually change to soft pink, then dark rose, and finally burgundy in the fall.

Both sedum and sempervivum like limestone but tolerate even acid soils. If you are preparing a container only for them, make sure it has good drainage, and mix crushed or broken brick, finely broken concrete or smashed pieces of plaster in with the potting mix. If you don't have any of these, purchased ground limestone will work just as well (but you lose the pleasure of recycling).

Shrubs and Trees

Many shrubs and trees are easily grown in containers. The area of the country you live in will determine which ones can be left outside year 'round. Few, if any, shrubs and trees will survive prolonged soil temperatures below 10°F. Above ground, in containers, their roots are much more exposed to cold than when planted in the ground. Shrubs and trees that will survive in the ground in cold zones will not necessarily survive in containers (see page 77 for how to save them over the winter).

Evergreens are nature's winter consolation to northern gardeners and what a consolation they are! Have you ever noticed the vast variety available? Evergreens may have broad, shiny leaves or dull, prickly, skinny needles, and they don't come only in green. They boast a wide range of winter color, from bronze, rust, mulberry, sea-green, gray, olive and deep green to gold. There are ever-

A ruffle of white impatiens surrounds the base of a pine tree.

Evergreens and ivy enclose a terrace at the top of a high-rise apartment building, giving privacy and shelter from the wind.

'Meyer's' lemon trees are a striking accent for the boxwood hedges in Cynthia Woodyard's garden.

RECOMMENDED TREES AND SHRUBS FOR GROWING IN CONTAINERS

COMMON NAME	LATIN NAME	MINIMUM CONTAINER SIZE FOR MATURE PLANT, WIDTH BY DEPTH
Alberta spruce	*Picea glauca* var. 'Albertiana'	24″ × 12″
Bean tree	*Laburnum alpinum* 'Pendulum'	24″ × 12″
Birch shrub	*Betula nana*	24″ × 12″
Blue mist spirea	*Caryopteris* × *clandonensis*	24″ × 12″
Boxwood	*Buxus sempervirens*	24″ × 12″
Broom	*Cytisus* × *beanii*	24″ × 12″
Broom	× *kewensis*	24″ × 12″
Broom	× *praecox*	24″ × 24″
Broom	*purpureus*	24″ × 18″
Butterfly bush	*Buddleia davidii*	36″ × 12″
Camellia	*Camellia* species	18″ × 18″
Cotoneaster	*Cotoneaster* species	24″ × 12″
Daphne	*Daphne collina*	24″ × 12″
Daphne	*Daphne mezereum*	24″ × 12″
Daphne	*Daphne tangutica*	24″ × 12″
Eucalyptus	*Eucalyptus* species	24″ × 12″
Fig tree	*Ficus* species	24″ × 12″
Golden bells	*Forsythia* species	24″ × 12″
Holly	*Ilex* species	24″ × 18″
Hydrangea	*Hydrangea arborescens*	24″ × 24″
Japanese andromeda	*Pieris japonica*	24″ × 12″
Japanese maple	*Acer palmatum* 'Dissectum'	36″ × 16″
Japanese maple	'Aureum'	36″ × 16″
Japanese maple	'Tricolor'	36″ × 16″
Jasmine	*Jasminum nudiflorum*	24″ × 12″
Laurel	*Kalmia latifolia*	24″ × 24″
Laurel, sweet bay	*Laurus nobilis*	24″ × 12″
Mimosa	*Albizia julibrissin*	24″ × 24″
Pittosporum	*Pittosporum tobira*	24″ × 12″
Purpleleaf sand cherry	*Prunus* × *cistena*	24″ × 12″
Rhododendron and azalea	*Rhododendron* species	24″ × 12″
St.-John's-wort	*Hypericum* species	24″ × 12″
Viburnum	*Viburnum* species	24″ × 16″
Weigela	*Weigela* species	24″ × 12″

greens with multicolored foliage, too, such as *Leucothoe fontanesiana* 'Rainbow'.

Conifers or cone-bearing evergreens tolerate root restrictions and are slower growing than other trees or shrubs, which makes them practical for containers. They are said to dislike pollution, but I've seen them grown beautifully in New York City, on high terraces where they have good air circulation. For those who like to prune, they can be shaped into globes, cones, spires or poodle variations with tufts or growths of ever-increasing larger balls rising up the trunk. Pines (*Pinus* species), yews (*Taxus* species), junipers and box (*Buxus sempervirens*) are all good choices, depending on where in the country you live. Junipers have blue to blue-gray foliage and a draping habit that can be very attractive in a container. One of most adaptable and cold hardy of the evergreen shrubs is the Alberta spruce (*Picea glauca*).

There are many spring-flowering shrubs, including azalea, rhododendron, forsythia and flowering almond. For colorful foliage and flowers grow *Hydrangea macrophylla* 'Tricolor'. Shrubs flowering in late summer include butterfly bush (*Buddleia* species), with fragrant lilaclike flowers in white, purple or pink; low-growing blue mist spirea (*Caryopteris* × *clandonensis*), with small blue flowers up and down their stems; and the chaste tree (*Vitex agnus castus*) with clustered blue flowers. If it's fall color you want, the dwarf Japanese maple, *Acer palmatum* 'Dissectum', has finely cut leaves that turn a frothy, bright orange-

red. For fragrance, the daphnes, lilacs and jasmines win hands down. Some varieties of daphnes, *Daphne caucasica*, for example, will flower for ten months straight outdoors in my Zone 7 garden, needing only a short rest. The flowers are small but their perfume is strong.

Many dwarf fruit trees can be grown as decorative container plants. Citrus fruits such as Ponderosa lemon, Meyer's lemon and Otaheite orange, to name a few, are often grown in pots. They can be wintered-over indoors in northern areas and summer in the garden. 'Meyer's', named after Frank N. Meyer, who first brought it out of China, is the most cold-hardy of the lemons and is probably the most popular. It is a small variety with almost thornless stems. The light orange oblong fruit is plentiful but not particularly good eating, as it is very acid. In a container, the plant can be stored in cool (just above freezing) place for the winter and placed outside for display the rest of the year.

When shrubs or trees are purchased it is easy to judge the size of the container needed. Some shrubs and trees are sold with their root balls wrapped in burlap. When placed in a container to "try it on for size," the container should be approximately a third larger than the root ball to give the roots enough soil to grow out into. Later, after the roots fill the container, the plant should be transplanted to the next largest size container, or, if you prefer that the shrub or tree remain a dwarf size, both the roots and the branches can

A grove of baytrees can be grown in tubs. In this formal garden they have been clipped into an umbrella shape.

be pruned yearly (see Pruning and Deadheading, page 75) and the plant can remain in the same container. It is as difficult to guess the mature size of a shrub or tree as it is to guess the mature size of a child. There are many gardening books that list an average height for shrubs and trees, but at best it is a guessing game. Who would be foolish enough to buy a suit for a child to wear when he is grown? The same principals hold for plants. Growth depends on many variables including parentage, nutrition and environment. The chart on the left will help you plan for a container before you purchase the plant. The dimensions are approximate.

Houseplants

Houseplants are more often grown for their decorative foliage than for their flowers. They are usually tolerant of low light or at least find a sunny window adequate. Some of the most popular houseplants are the "wandering" plants, plants that have

long, trailing stems and are easily propagated from cuttings because the nodes (where the leaves join that stem) easily root. Some plants send out roots into the air from nodes and there miniature plants quickly form, providing an impressive supply for the gardener and friends of baby plants that can be cut from the mother and planted into the soil. (Keep in mind that generosity with plants always repays the giver. As Sir Peter Smithers, world-renowned horticulturist, says, "The pleasure of owning a fine plant is not complete until it has been given to friends.") Strawberry geranium (*Saxifraga stolonifera*), spider plant (*Chlorophytum comosum* 'Vittatum') and Wandering Jew (*Zebrina pendula* and *Tradescantia* species both have the common name of Wandering Jew) are some of the most popular wandering plants; all are usually considered houseplants, but no matter, they have wonderful foliage and easily grow as outdoor container plants.

Strawberry geraniums have deep green leaves, brightly variegated due to their silvery veins. The underside of the leaves and the stalks are a dull red, making the plant showy whether in bloom or not. 'Tricolor' has red, white and green leaves. In spring 1-foot-high stalks covered with many tiny flowers rise above the foliage and stay in bloom for several months.

The easy-to-grow spider plants have arching narrow leaves with white or yellow stripes down their centers. In summer they send out arching flower stalks, often as long as 40 inches. Small star-shaped white flowers form along with baby plants or plantlets, giving rise to another common name, throw the children out the window. Wandering Jew (*Tradescantia fluminensis variegata*), with fleshy leaves stained purple and banded with creamy white and pale yellow, is a foliage plant that enhances the green of any plant it sits next to. Many flowering plants are at their best when surrounded by foliage plants, which draw attention to the blooms by providing a background.

Cuttings can be taken from foliage houseplants in early February to grow on indoors until they can be planted safely outdoors in containers. Any houseplant will enjoy a vacation outdoors if moved out when the temperatures outside are close to the temperatures inside.

Top: *Annuals (red salvia, dwarf morning glory, pink and rose geranium) combine well with the Wandering Jew* (Tradescantia) *usually grown as a houseplant.* Bottom: *Even a shaded entrance can be filled with color. Pots of red begonia and white-flowering Tahitian bridal veil* (Spathiphyllum) *create a bright welcome.*

Vines and Creepers

Vines, the most forgotten plants in gardening, happily can tie the diverse plants in a container or a container garden together. Vines are a large and assorted group of individuals with different behaviors; there are the drapers, the clingers, the grabbers, the floppers, the gropers, the tailers and the tumblers. Some are loose stemmed and happy-go-lucky, while others are stiff and difficult. Some of the stronger vines can be caught on their way up to act as a trellis for other, more delicate, vines.

Vines fall into three categories: those that need to be fastened to their supports, those that climb by means of twining stems or tendrils, and those that anchor themselves by means of little "suction cups" or holdfasts. Before planting a vine in a container, it is important to understand its behavior and whether it will need a trellis or a wall to climb, or if it can arch gracefully and spill down the sides of a container.

Ivies are hard to beat as companions that enhance flowering plants. Even when planted alone in a container they bring a bit of green color and life to dim, poorly lighted areas. Ivies have small aerial roots that cling tenaciously to whatever they touch, making them easy to train into topiaries, to climb walls or to drape over containers. There are many different ivies from which to choose. English ivies (*Hedera helix*) alone are available in more than 60 varieties, with lobed, round or heart-shaped leaves, and smooth, ruffled, wavy or curled edges. Try the

Vines grown in pots, such as this morning glory, can be placed to grow up into a flowering camouflage, in this case to conceal a drainpipe.

Four pots of ivy, trained in cone shapes and strategically placed, create vertical posts to separate the seating area from the rest of the terrace.

glossy-leaved grape ivy (*Cissus rhombifolia*), with 4-inch-long, three-lobed leaves that are bronze colored when new and slowly change to green, or the large-leaved (5 to 7 inches across) variegated Algerian ivy (*Hedera canariensis* 'Variegata'), with its gray-green leaves edged with blotches of white and distinctive wine-red twigs and stems.

Vinca (*Vinca major* 'Variegata') looks a little like ivy. It is a tender-leaved vine that will be killed by freezing temperatures but can be saved indoors as a houseplant over the winter. Each leaf is edged with a whitish-yellow rim that sparkles in the sunlight. It grows considerably faster than ivy. By summer's end, if conditions are favorable, second-story window boxes planted with vinca have vines that reach the ground, like

Vinca (Vinca major 'Variegata') is a fast-growing vine. With favorable conditions this plant nearly reaches the ground by summer's end.

A metal cone-shaped treillage is placed on top of a pot for mandevilla vine to twist around as it grows. The base of the pot is seeded with sweet alyssum.

Rapunzel letting down her hair. (One summer our second-story window box sent vinca down in a curtain over the kitchen door, and we had to part the vines to walk in and out. I was reminded of the Chinese beaded curtains that give privacy to mysterious back rooms.)

Annual vines can be grown from seed to flower within a season. They reach their mature heights in a very short time. Black-eyed Susan vine (*Thunbergia alata*), a lively climber for a hanging basket, has arrowhead-shaped leaves and soft yellow, white or orange daisy flowers with round, dark, unblinking eyes peeking out. It will grow up and twine around a hanging basket's wires, reaching for the ceiling while, at the same time,

gallantly reach down to hide the basket's bare bottom. Black-eyed Susan vine quickly grows 5- to 6-foot-long stems, blooming as it goes, as early as 60 days from sowing. It has a mind of its own and doesn't like to be pruned or shaped while it is blooming, so let it wander as it will, and make room for its long stems.

The longer-growing annual vines of morning glories, moonflowers and canary creepers are not complicated to grow, either. Plant the seeds in a peat pot indoors before the last frost and move them into a larger container and outdoors a few weeks after the last frost when the nights have warmed to 55° to 60° F. The peat pot can be planted directly into a larger

container without disturbing the vine's roots; the container can then be placed next to an existing structure the vine can climb on, such as a railing, a banister, a drain pipe or a column.

Morning glories and moonflowers are two of my favorite vines to grow together in the same container. They are like an old married couple compatible because one works nights and the other works days. The morning glory opens with the first bright sunshine and closes at twilight. The moonflower opens as the afternoon wanes and, for a few glorious hours the two vines party together. The 'Heavenly Blue' morning glory and the bright white moonflower complement each other, forming a design as timeless as that of delft china. As if that isn't enough, the powerful fragrance of the moonflower rates as one of nature's best.

Tropical vines, among them passionflower, bougainvillea and dipladenia, are slower growing than such annual vines as morning glories and moonflowers, but flower all summer and can be wintered-over in a sunny window facing south. Bougainvillea in any of its glowing neon colors of flamingo pink, passionate purple and outrageous orange is a neck-jerker; you can't pass it without turning your head to stare. This is not a plant for the timid, unless you choose a bright white which becomes a soft beacon at night. Every statement bougainvillea makes is excessive. When it flowers, it puts out so many blossoms it is hard to see the leaves. The colorful part of the plant is really the papery bracts that surround the actual tiny creamy yellow flowers. Its popularity stems in part from the fact that most of the time it cares for itself, liking to dry out between waterings, tolerating drought for brief periods. Once established, bougainvillea prefers its roots crowded in a pot and rests all winter, requiring only a temperature of 46° to 54°, no food, and little water. When nights reach 60° F it can be moved outdoors. The two basics to bear in mind are to keep the stems pruned back to three or four feet long to prevent the plant from producing sharp thorns, and wrap it in full sun daily during the summer. Originally from Brazil, bougainvillea is now common in the southern states, where it scrambles along highways, climbs arbors and paints the landscape with blatant colors that can be seen for miles in any direction.

I prefer dipladenia's (*Mandevilla sanderi*) long-lasting trumpet-shaped flowers that grow in clusters of softer shades of pink or white. It is a slow grower, with a shrubby shape until it ages. Then it grows with long, climbing stems that can reach 15 feet. For the container gardener, slow growth can be a plus. Slow-growing plants seldom need repotting or pruning. If pruning dipladenia, do so right after the plant stops flowering. Each year's flowers are produced on new growth, so if you prune the new stems, you won't have flowers the following summer. Dipladenia can be trained to grow on a wire hoop or a small trellis. Indoors, it needs warm (60° F) and humid air. Misting or placing dipla-

denia on a saucer filled with gravel and water helps keep the air around it moist.

Some vining vegetables are excellent to grow for decoration and amusement. Tiny 'Jack Be Little' pumpkins, 2 to 4 inches across, look whimsical hanging from a 5-foot-long vine on a terrace—reason enough to grow them. Scarlet runner bean was not only popular with the colonists for its beans and its tolerance of cold soil, allowing it to be planted early, but also for its bright red, sweet-pea-like flowers that continue blooming until well after the first frost. Hyacinth bean is another decorative vine grown for its light pink, sweet-pea-like flowers that contrast sharply against deep purple bean pods. The bean pods are edible but are grown more often for decoration. Both hyacinth and scarlet runner beans can grow 10-plus feet a season, so they need a large pot and a support around which to twine.

Baby's tears (*Soleirolia soleirolii*) is a low creeper with tear-shaped leaves and blooms almost too small to see. It never draws attention to itself. This may sound as though it has little to recommend it, but there's more. It forms a perfect carpet of neat, minute foliage, almost a doll house miniature plant, that continues to spread. A small clump can quickly cover the soil under an upright plant in a container and, before you know it, cascade down the sides. It is shallow-rooted, and so to transplant it, I reach into the pot usually without a trowel and gently lift a clump, lay it in another pot to hide bare soil,

---

VINES FOR CONTAINERS

COMMON NAME	LATIN NAME
Allamanda	*Allamanda cathartica*
Baby winter creeper	*Euonymus fortunei* 'Minima'
Baby's tears	*Soleirolia soleirolii*
Balloon vine	*Cardiospermum halicacabum*
Black-eyed Susan vine	*Thunbergia alata*
Bleeding heart vine	*Clerodendrum thomsoniae*
Bougainvillea	*Bougainvillea glabra*
Clematis	*Clematis* species
Cup-and-saucer vine	*Cobaea scandens*
Dipladenia	*Mandevilla sanderi*
Dipladenia	*Mandevilla splendens*
English ivy	*Hedera helix*
Hyacinth bean	*Dolichos lablab*
Ivy geranium	*Pelargonium peltatum*
Jasmine	*Jasminum* species
Moonflower	*Ipomoea alba*
Morning glory	*Ipomoea purpurea*
Nasturtium	*Tropaeolum majus*
Passionflower	*Passiflora* species
Porcelain berry	*Ampelopsis brevipedunculata* 'Elegans'
Scarlet runner bean	*Phaseolus coccineus*
Swedish ivy	*Plectranthus australis*
Sweet pea	*Lathyrus odoratus*
Variegated Algerian ivy	*Hedera canariensis* 'Variegata'

water it in and watch it perform. It prefers a fairly moist soil and bright light, but not burning sun. It works its magic wherever it goes, flattering the plants whose feet it covers, making them seem more at home in their containers and ultimately more beautiful.

A simple but beautiful topiary can be made with baby's tears. Fill three progressively smaller terra-cotta pots with soil. (Use plastic pots if you like, but terra cotta is inexpensive and prettier.) Place the middle-sized pot in the center of the larger pot and the smaller pot in the center of the middle-sized pot, making sure there is at least a 2-inch ring of soil exposed at the edge of each pot. This is where the baby's tears will be planted. As it grows it will cascade over the sides and down the pots, in time completely covering the pots. Baby's tears happily covers any shape.

Roses

Roses are undeniably difficult, but in spite of their tantrums they are America's most popular plant. No matter what their size, they are usually the center of attention wherever they are. Like prima donnas, they expect special attention. At times they give seemingly contradictory signals. They require a lot of water and yet they don't want their feet to stay wet. They are heavy feeders and could be liquid-fertilized almost every time they are watered, but given too much fertilizer they become stingy with their blooms.

Roses boast a large family with many stars. To complicate the matter, roses fall into many categories. A simple list includes hybrid tea roses, floribunda roses, grandiflora roses, climbers, tree roses, shrub roses, old roses and miniature roses. Considerations in choosing a

rose are disease resistance, fragrance, stem length, duration of bloom (some bloom in early summer and some all summer), height and the amount of care you will be able to give. Some, as is the case with most hybrid tea roses, require weekly spraying with a fungicide to prevent black spot and look their best. Others, shrub and old roses for the most part, need less care. A soilless potting mix will avoid fungal disease that hides in garden soil. The size of the pot needed varies with the type of rose to be grown. Hybrid tea and larger shrub roses need at least a 14-inch-deep, 18-inch-wide pot. Miniature roses can be grown in small pots 6 inches deep and 10 inches in diameter.

Miniature roses are the most adaptable group and can be grown over the winter as houseplants in a sunny window. They are easiest in northern gardens because they are content to continue their bloom indoors. The larger rosebushes are more difficult to bring indoors. Depending on the rose and your growing zone, many types can remain outdoors year 'round. Above Zone 7 it is doubtful that they can survive without winter protection. When the temperature drops below 28°F container-grown roses should be moved into an unheated shelter. Roses that have been grafted are not as hardy as roses that are grown on their own roots.

In the place of a railing, pots of roses and hibiscus border the edge of this large deck.

Ask Yourself When Selecting Plants

1. How long do I want to have bloom?

2. Will the plant have sun or shade?

3. Do I want to save the plant from one season to the next?

4. Will I be using the area with the containers in the evening? If so, do I want flowers that will stay open at night? Should I use white flowers that hold the light at night and are easier to see?

5. What colors exist in the area where I want the containers? Flower colors should be coordinated with the colors of surrounding furniture, walls and the like as well as with the colors of the container itself.

6. What is the size of the full-grown plant? Will it have room for its mature roots in the container? How will the proportions of the plant fit with the pot? Will it be so large the pot looks top heavy, or so small the pot looks more important than the plant?

7. Is fragrance a consideration?

The color and fragrance of a rose garden offer a feast for the senses. An urn filled with lamb's ears and miniature roses is set in the center of this garden, where several paths lined with sweet-smelling lavender all come together.

THE CONTAINER PLANTING AND GROWING GUIDE

CHOOSING A CONTAINER

Containers may be as traditional as clay pots, half barrels, urns, wooden boxes, hanging baskets, window boxes and wheelbarrows, and as unconventional as tree stumps, rubber tires, bird cages, bathtubs and old rowboats. Almost as many different kinds of containers have been used to hold flowers as there are flowers to grow. I've seen a great deal of imagination and humor in the selection of containers across America, which have included a life-size, wooden cut-out of a cow carrying real flowers on its back, and a broken-down wicker chair with flowers growing where the seat used to be. Recycled or "found" objects have long been popular with gardeners. Old shoes, coffee cans, chimney-flue tiles, wheelbarrows, wagons and buckets are often used. What's important is not what the container is but whether it is clean, able to hold soil and water and will fit into its surroundings. Containers without drainage holes can be used, but good results are more difficult to obtain; if possible, add a few drainage holes, for drainage is essential to successful container gardening. You take it from there and use your imagination.

Heavy containers can be placed on casters or plant dollies for easy moving. If the plants are getting more sun and growing better on one side of the container, castors make it easier to rotate. Move your containers around to bring a particularly attractive one into a position of prominence for the fullest enjoyment of its display. Weight isn't a consideration for small containers set on the ground, but it is for hanging baskets and large containers on decks or balconies. Even a lightweight container, once filled with an artificial soil, can be heavy when watered; a planted 25-gallon container, the size of a large garbage can, can weigh more than 200 pounds.

Here are some of the most commonly used containers and their advantages:

A simple yet sophisticated planting of variegated ivy, strategically placed in the center of a shady lawn, is a sculptural and attractive accent.

TERRA-COTTA CONTAINERS. Terra-cotta pots are inexpensive, attractive and porous. This material allows water to leach out, and air to pass through, too. As a result, more frequent watering may be necessary. Aged terra-cotta are more attractive than new, with interesting white patches. If a terra-cotta container is left in a shady, moist spot, moss and lichen will grow in attractive green patches on the surface.

Terra-cotta pots may be ornate or plain, and come in great

Rosalind Creasy welcomes visitors with a walk through a flower garden instead of the more traditional front lawn. A whimsical hen terra-cotta planter sits on the front step growing hens and chicks (Sempervivum tectorum).

variety from the classic round shapes with pie crust rims to squares and animal shapes. There are metal feet and saucers available to set the pot off the ground for better drainage and air circulation. Heavy metal clip-on hangers are available that attach under the rim of the pot to allow it to be wall mounted, hung from a ceiling or attached to railings. Remember that the pot can be very heavy depending on its size, the type of soil used and the amount of water it holds.

A disadvantage of terra-cotta is that it is fragile and can be chipped or broken. In northern gardens it can't be left out in the winter because freezing and thawing will cause cracking.

METAL CONTAINERS. Metal conducts heat readily and so can overheat tender roots. Rust can be another problem, especially if it leaches into the soil where it can poison the plant. Many metal planters are fitted with a plastic liner to insulate the roots from overheating and protect the plant from rust.

PRESSED-FIBER CONTAINERS. Lightweight, attractive copies of cement urns are available, and so true in appearance that they're hard to tell from the real thing once they are planted. The soil will dry out faster in pressed-fiber containers than in wooden containers.

WOODEN CONTAINERS. Wood can be heavy. The larger containers tend to become permanent fixtures on a terrace or balcony. They are simple to construct, and many a do-it-yourselfer has made his or her own. Wood helps insulate plant roots

from heat stress caused by solar radiation, and when a wooden container is painted a light color, it deflects radiation and absorbs even less heat. Wood also allows air to reach the roots, essential for good growth.

Different woods have different characteristics. The best for containers are cypress, teak, cedar and redwood, because their natural oils make them resistant to rotting. Other, less rot-resistant wood, such as pine, can be used but should first be treated with a nontoxic preservative, such as is used for greenhouse benches.

SELF-WATERING CONTAINERS. There are many different designs of self-watering containers available with built-in water reservoirs that only require refilling weekly. They have a capillary wick system that allows the plant to draw up water as needed. Rubbermaid Inc.'s Anywhere Garden, and Mantis Manufacturing Gardengrid, among others, make good, protective, self-watering containers.

CONCRETE CONTAINERS. Concrete planters are attractive but very heavy. This is an advantage if you're worried about theft, but a disadvantage if you want to be able to move them. Cement contains lime, which leaches into the soil when the plants are watered. If you're growing acid-loving plants, it is better first to paint the inside of the planter with foundation coating to keep the lime from your plants.

PLASTIC POTS. Plastic pots are inexpensive and lightweight. Water doesn't evaporate through the plastic as it does with terra-cotta. I prefer the dark green or black pots as they don't distract from the flowers the way the stark white pots do. Plastic pots can be placed inside more decorative containers such as wooden window boxes and terra-cotta pots to help hold in more water in hot climates and to make it easy to change the flowers seasonally. They can also be reused for many years. Before reusing, be sure to wash the pot with household bleach diluted with 10 parts water to kill any bacteria left by the previous occupant. Always use a new sterile growing medium each time you plant.

FIBERGLASS CONTAINERS. Fiberglass containers are expensive but durable impostors that are hard to distinguish from wooden planters unless touched. They are lightweight and easy to move, or even attach to the side of a house as window boxes.

They need only a good hosing to clean them. They tend to dry out faster than wooden containers.

BASKETS. Baskets tend to rot quickly unless lined with plastic to prevent contact with water and soil. I have many baskets that I have reused from year to year, protecting them from water by lining them with plastic. Many eventually lose their bottoms to rot, but when set on the ground this doesn't show, and they're still attractive and useful for hiding plastic pots.

CHIMNEY FLUES AND CONCRETE BUILDING BLOCKS. These are inexpensive and behave like terra-cotta except that they are bottomless. (Chimney flues look like terra-cotta, too.) They are perfect for placing on a gravel driveway, stone terrace or anywhere they won't be damaged by direct contact with soil or ground water.

With the addition of a wooden box, an old wheelbarrow has been turned into a planter. Each compartment holds a different variety of sedum.

A poured-cement swan planter has petunias for tail feathers and blue lobelias for wings. In hot weather it will need to be watered daily.

DRAINAGE

To grow properly, plants, like humans, need air, water and nutrients. Each of these must be readily available in the soil where the plant can make use of it. Good drainage allows excess water to drain quickly and air to remain between the soil particles. That's why it is best for each container to have a drainage hole in the bottom to allow water to exit the pot. Sometimes this isn't possible; some of the more decorative pots aren't made with drainage holes and would be ruined if you tried to make holes in them. The best solution is to place another pot,

one size smaller and with a drainage hole, inside the decorative container. Propped up a little from the bottom with pebbles, it will allow water to drain properly.

For all pots, even those with drainage holes, it is imperative to put a few inches of coarse material in the bottom to promote drainage. Broken terra-cotta pottery and gravel are commonly used, and white Styrofoam peanuts (packing material) will work too. While the Styrofoam peanuts are an environmental nightmare (they don't break down when added to land

fill), we can make a bad situation better by "recycling" and using them in the bottom of large containers. The peanuts can fill the bottom third or half of the barrel, depending on your choice of plants and how deep their roots grow. In the deeper barrels a sheet of screen placed on top of the Styrofoam peanuts will prevent soil from sifting down into the cracks between them to create a solid plug at the bottom. A lightweight planting medium placed on top of peanuts will make for a lighter, easier to move container.

It is best if containers are

A stone pig wallows in the shade of an antique cart filled with pots of geraniums and ivy. The cart and pig are appropriately placed at an entrance to horse stables.

A wooden wheelbarrow planted with flowers is placed alongside a garden, looking as though the gardener were about to return and plant them.

Connie Cross filled an antique baby carriage with browallia and left it parked as a pleasant surprise for visitors to find along a shady woodland walk.

elevated a few inches off the ground (or other surface) so water can drain out and away. Saucers and plant stands are available that actually hold the container up. There are also iron stands with feet, which are decorative and whimsical. Even an upside-down terra-cotta pot can make a decorative stand—just use something to keep the bottom of the container from resting flush against the surface.

POTTING SOIL

Good soil preparation ensures the provision of nutrients for the growing plant. When you are planting a container garden you aren't obliged to amend existing soil as you do in the garden, but can simply buy a specially formulated soil mix balanced in nutrients and with fertilizer and good drainage built in. Such potting materials not only promote good plant growth but are relatively lightweight, an important plus for container gardening. Pots, boxes and hanging baskets can be heavy to move around or suspend and are much easier to handle when weight is kept to a minimum. You should, however, install large containers in their permanent homes before filling and planting them.

If you're tempted to use garden soil in your containers because it is close at hand and costs nothing, think again. Garden soil is not sterile and contains weed seed, insects and perhaps a fungus or two. Garden soil frequently lacks many of the necessary nutrients for healthy growth, which are needed all the more in a container where plants must grow closer together. Furthermore, every time you water plants in a container, nutrients leach out of the soil; the plants' roots can't extend their search for nutrients outside the container. Do yourself a favor. Save time and later aggravation by using a good prepared soil in your containers. Good potting soil is essential for containers and it is inexpensive. Plants potted up with a sterile potting soil have a better start on life than plants grown in a garden.

There are many different varieties of mix on the market. Some products should be moistened before the plants are added. Some, like Pro Mix, are composed of horticultural sphagnum moss, equal parts of horticultural vermiculite and perlite, together with ingredients to sustain initial plant growth. Before filling the containers, Pro Mix needs to be thoroughly wetted by turning the mix while spraying with water. Wetting the mix facilitates water absorption and distribution. There are other good mixes available (Sunshine is one) which can be planted and watered afterward. Before you plant, read the directions carefully. Because over- or under-watering can be a serious problem, it is important to have a soilless mix that absorbs and holds water without drowning the plants. Many of the potting mixes sold for containers contain moisture-holding material. Check whether the plants you have selected prefer acid or alkaline soil, and purchase the appropriate soil mix. Coordinate the fertilizer you use with the plant's needs by choosing one for acid-loving or alkaline-loving plants. Most plants require a soil that is slightly acid. If you need a lime soil, a few pieces of broken cement mixed in the soil will leach some lime into the soil every time it is watered.

If you are planting quite a number of containers and prefer to make your own potting mix, a good formula for most plants is equal parts compost, sharp (or "builder's") sand and good loamy soil. Be sure the sand is not from a saltwater beach; salt residue in beach sand is harmful to plants. Sharp sand is available from building suppliers. Perlite or vermiculite may be substituted for the sand.

When potting, the soil line should be at least an inch below the rim of the container, several inches in the case of half barrels or larger containers. This will prevent soil from washing out of the container when it is watered, dirtying the area around it. This becomes even more important if the planter is placed where heavy, drenching rains might fall.

Whether you are transplanting seedlings or fully grown plants, first moisten the soil in the container, then rap the bottom of the container on a flat surface to loosen the plant. Hold the plant upside down and gently remove it, soil and all. Next, before planting, loosen the soil around the roots by pressing with your thumbs on the bottom and gently pulling the soil outward to expose the roots. You want the roots to grow out into the soil in the new pot, not keep the shape of the pot from which they are being removed. When transplanting be careful not to damage the tiny white root hairs. Gently firm the soil around the base of the plant. Make sure it is planted at soil level, not rounded above the soil and the pot. This will cause water to run off the plant, wetting the surface rather than soaking it.

STAKING

To stake or not to stake is a question of style, taste and time. Sometimes staking is only a matter of appearance, helpful if the plant looks messy sprawling over its neighbor. Sometimes staking is necessary for the plant's health, if the flowers are rotting on the ground or the plant is leaning too heavily on and suffocating its neighbor. Plants usually survive in the wild without staking, but some of the hybridized plants bred to grow numerous flowers or larger flower heads need help to stand up. Some plants have a single heavy flower head that needs support. Lilies and delphiniums are good examples. A stake the same thickness as the mature stem, placed a few inches from the stem, will support the stem and the flower if secured in several places with a soft string that won't cut into the stem. Plant ties may be wire, coated wire, twine, plastic tape, rubber strap, strips of cloth or old nylon stockings. The choice depends on the purpose. Wire can cut right through a plant stem in a good wind or if secured too tightly. Cloth or twine will hold without cutting. Wire itself makes a fine trellis, one many vines twine and hold onto by themselves. If you don't want to bother with staking, buy dwarf varieties; in the case of vines, plant them next to an existing structure they can twine about (pole, railing, drainpipe—see pages 61–64 for more information).

If you know your plants will need stakes, the best time to put them in is when you plant. Tie the plant loosely to the stake as soon as it is tall enough—a foot high, or when it starts to lean. This way the plant's roots will not be injured when you jab the plant stake (or stakes) into the container, and the plant will be trained to grow straight from the beginning. Stake with premade wire cages or hoops on tripod legs by placing them over the plants early on, so the plant can grow up through the cage; if a cage or hoop is placed on too late, flowers and stems will be broken as they are forced through the opening. Requirements for staking are individual. Most plants are best served by stakes one-third shorter than the plant's mature size, so the stakes are hidden by the foliage and flower heads. A few fast-growing plants such as tomatoes and vines need supports that are taller and stronger. (Large wooden planters for growing vines can have a trellis nailed to the inside back wall before the soil and plants are added.)

Hoops can be made at home from wire coat hangers, then attached to a stake or stakes to support a small plant. For this it is best to use coated metal that won't rust or corrode. If a plant is overgrown and starting to flop, a quick fix with bamboo poles and green twine will prop it up. Any stakes painted green will naturally blend with the foliage and not distract from the

A large terra-cotta planter accents the corner of a pool. Morning glories and ivy are planted to grow down the sides. Lantana will grow up right into a mound on the top.

plant. The bamboo poles are cut to just below the flower heads, allowing 4 to 6 inches for underground placement. The number of poles used depends on the circumference of the plant. For most smaller plants four will do. The poles should circle the plant. Twine is then wrapped around each pole and on to the next, several times around the circumference of the plant, as a sort of corral.

A rectangular planter can hold a living screen to shade an area or provide privacy. Be-fore planting mix is added to the box, an upright board is nailed onto the outside of each small end. Several horizontal poles or wires are attached be-tween the two supports at 8- to 10-inch intervals. The height of the upright boards depends on the type of vines you're grow-ing; 4 feet is a minimum. An-other approach is to nail a store-bought trellis to the back of the box. This works if the box is to be placed against a wall that will help support the trellis when the vines grow heavy.

A LIVING SCREEN

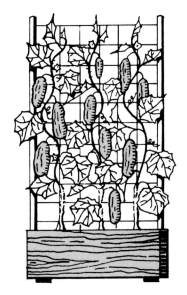

A box 3 feet long, 11 inches wide and deep will accommodate three cucumber plants on a 3-foot trellis.

SPACING PLANTS

Space your container plants closer together than you would in a garden. With good soil, a deep pot and weekly liquid fer-tilizing, you can grow many plants in a small area. An 8-inch hanging basket can hold three to five young plants, while a 10-inch hanging basket will hold five to seven. If you are filling your basket with small rooted cuttings, you can use more: three to five for a 6-inch pot, five to seven for an 8-inch pot, and seven to nine for a 10-inch pot. If your plants are in full bloom and you're moving them into a large container, it is easy to see the size of the roots and judge the area they need from that. They can be placed only a few inches apart if the container is deep enough to give the roots growing space.

WATERING

The biggest disadvantages to a container garden are that con-tainers dry out much faster than a "real" garden does, and the plant roots are more exposed to heat and cold because they are above ground. In containers, plants are planted closer together than in a garden and they all need to share in the water. The leaves tend to be more exposed to wind, so moisture is lost through transpiration. Fortunately, by using the latest garden products and technology we can handle these problems. Special polymers are readily and cheaply available and, when mixed with your planting medium, vastly increase water retention; special granules absorb many times their volume in water, and turn into a gel that slowly and steadily releases the water as needed. Although you still have to water, this relieves you of frequent watering while at the same time protecting the plant from overwatering.

Overwatering is the number-one cause of container plant mortality. When a plant is overwatered, the problem doesn't show up until several days later, when the leaves yellow, rot and fall off. Often it is too late to save the plant. To determine if a plant is too soggy stick a finger into the soil. Don't water if the soil is wet below the surface.

These simple rules will help prevent problems when watering your plants:

1. Whenever possible, plant in a pot with a drainage hole in the bottom.
2. Water thoroughly and allow the water to drain out the bottom of the pot. Never let water sit in a saucer under a plant.
3. When you have to use a pot without a drainage hole, fill the bottom one to two inches of the pot with gravel, broken pieces of clay pot, pebbles, shells or other coarse material before filling it with your planting medium. This provides a place for the water to drain so the soil will not retain the water and drown the roots.

4. Never water without feeling the soil first to make sure it is dry to the touch. Some plants like to dry out briefly between watering.
5. If containers are placed in an exceptionally windy area or an exceptionally hot area, they will bake. The soil and the plants will need more attention and more water.
6. Wash plants weekly if they are not being washed by rainfall.
7. Use a rose attachment for a watering can or a fine-spray nozzle on a hose to trickle or sprinkle water gently into a container. Strong jets of water can disturb and damage plant roots.
8. A fine mulch can prevent erosion and keep weeds from growing. In the case of a long-lived plant and a mulch that breaks down relatively rapidly, this can add nutrients to the soil.
9. Use water-retaining polymer in the soil, which will help to hold moisture and yet protect the plant from overwatering.

A drip irrigation system can be handy for managing a large number of containers. These systems have thin flexible tubes, usually dark in color to prevent algae growth and to make them easier to hide. They can be run unobtrusively along a fence or wall from the source of water to the containers. Smaller tubes run from the larger main tube into the individual containers where water is dripped slowly to soak the soil surrounding the roots. The tubes are held in place by pins. An advantage of the drip system is that less water is used and, consequently, less water is wasted. And if the tube is buried below ground or

hidden by mulch, even less water will be lost to evaporation.

Should you have to be away for a week or two, containers can be prepared to water themselves. Pots can be placed in a cool, shaded place so they will need less water. (For sunny plants, this will slow their growth.) An improvised system for drip watering the plants through a fiber wick, available at garden centers and hardware stores, can be set up. A pot of water is placed on a stand above the containers to be watered; the wick is anchored under water with a small weight. The other end of the wick is anchored the same way beneath the soil of the plant to be watered. Water will be drawn into the drying container.

If after all your attention you find a wilted plant, take heart: There are revival techniques. Some plants need only a good drink and perhaps to be set on a saucer filled with gravel and water. The gravel lifts the plant above the water so the plants roots are not sitting in it. As the water evaporates, the plant will revive quickly as its leaves are surrounded with humidity from the evaporating water. Nearly dried-out plants, where the soil has visibly shrunk from the sides of the container, will need to be submerged in water deeper than the rim of the pot. As the soil soaks up the badly needed moisture, air bubbles will rise to the surface. The plant should remain under water until the bubbles stop coming. This could be a half hour or longer. Then the plant is removed from the water and allowed to drain.

MULCH

In the case of container plants enjoyed up close, it detracts from the beauty of the plant to see the soil. An attractive way to hide the soil is with mulch. A good mulch will hold moisture in the soil, cutting down on evaporation, and will keep the plant's roots cool. Mulches may be organic or shallow-rooted, living plants.

Select mulch carefully so it blends in visually with the plant. Small-scale mulches are best in containers; the more common garden mulches of shredded leaves, large bark or wood chips aren't very attractive here. Organic mulches that are good-looking are chopped pine needles and coco hulls. (The one drawback—or advantage, depending on whether you're di-eting or not—is that new coconut hulls have a rich chocolate color and an aroma that will linger for a week or two.) A fine gravel is recommended for succulents, making them look more at home in a dry place, but it is distracting at the base of other plants. Spanish moss or decorative floral moss is frequently used by florists for dressing up a plant. Either can be purchased by the home gardener and are attractive on most plants. There are many imaginative possibilities. If you are growing evergreens, pinecones could be used as mulch, adding a decorative touch.

Some shallow-rooted plants can act as living mulches to keep roots cool and hold the moisture. The best plants for this give the lush effect of a soft draping of green. On the other hand, some plants are admired not for their great beauty but for their strength of character, their helpful nature and undemanding ways. Baby's tears is one of these. It works well under standard-grown plants (see page 63 and "A Soft Touch" below) and makes friends wherever it goes.

There are other plants that will hide the soil at the base of potted plants, depending on the depth of the plant's roots. Larger plants can have their bases covered by ivy, spider plants, creeping fig, strawberry geraniums and others. Experiment and learn by doing. You'll discover that most of nature's plants are flexible.

A Soft Touch

Baby's tears is never competitive, always compatible. The tiny leaves of creeping baby's tears are a lovely way to hide the soil at the base of trees and shrubs (ficus, hibiscus and oleander come immediately to mind) and even upright flowering plants such as flowering maple benefit from a cloud of baby's tears at their base. Baby's tears is shallow-rooted, spreads quickly and drapes softly over the rims of pots. It is also a good indicator that the container needs water, signaling this when its bright green color fades. Years ago I started with one small pot of baby's tears. I clumsily pulled it apart when unpotting it to plant it at the base of a ficus tree and discovered even little sections are easily and successfully repotted. Now, any time I need baby's tears, I pull up a small section with my fingers, pat it on top of loose soil, water it in and, like magic, a living green rug grows in the shade of a larger plant.

FERTILIZER

Every time plants are watered, nutrients wash out of the soil, making it necessary to feed container plants on a regular basis. There are many types of fertilizer available, but the most practical are water-soluble, which go directly to the plant's roots, and the slow-release, which remains in the soil for months, releasing the fertilizer when the plants are watered. A liquid fertilizer, if watered-in deeply, goes directly to the plant roots and is easy for the plant to absorb quickly. However, it doesn't stay long in the soil. The slow-release fertilizers are available in various forms: plant sticks, pellets and granules. Any of the fertilizers available for houseplants will do the job. Compared to garden fertilizer, they are usually high in phosphorus, for strong root growth, and lower in nitrogen and potassium. A discoloration of leaves is a sign of overfeeding or underfeeding. A phosphorus deficiency causes a purplish coloring on the underside of the leaves, and a nitrogen deficiency is evident by a yellowing on the top of the leaves. A brown edge signals a potassium deficiency or a build-up of salt in the soil. Nitrogen promotes growth of green stems and leaves, and potassium helps the plant manufacture sugar and starches, as well as aiding in their transport throughout the plant. For a container-grown plant, strong root growth is more important than it is for a garden-grown plant.

It is important to apply fertilizer according to the manufacturer's directions. Never use more fertilizer than the recommended dosage. Next to overwatering, overfertilizing kills more container plants. A build-up of harmful fertilizer salts is easily recognized by a white crust on the soil or the sides of a pot or burnt leaf margins, especially leaf tips. To correct this situation the plant can be immersed in a pail of tepid water for a half hour, or held under running water for several minutes to leach out the salts. Many container plants brought inside for the winter will need a rest period (see page 79) and should not be fertilized until it is time for spring growth. A seedling should be fertilized only after it reaches three to four inches in height, and a cutting, when it starts new growth.

If your plants appear to be growing too slowly, or come under an attack by pests or disease, you may want to treat them to the quick method of absorption to rally their strength. Use a liquid fertilizer that can be used as foliar spray at half strength, and spray it directly on the leaves, which will absorb it immediately. The plant leaves send the nutrition to the roots for added vigor.

CAUTION: Overfeeding overencourages foliage at the expense of flowers. If you use powdered fertilizers, keep them away from stems, leaves and roots. Moisten the soil before adding powdered fertilizers to avoid "burning" the plant.

PRUNING AND DEADHEADING

Pruning for most container plants means pinching, deadheading or disbudding. For many plants, removing faded flowers and seed-pods will increase the number of flowers and extend the season of bloom. Plants perpetuate their species by developing a profusion of seeds. To accomplish this, they must first produce flowers. Many plants will stay in flower longer if the flower blossoms are deadheaded or pinched off before they start forming seed. Once the plant starts to produce seeds, it will produce fewer and fewer flowers. Ripening seed produce hormones that depress flower production; when you pinch off the flower blossoms early, the plant's entire store of energy is directed to producing new flowers. There are plants that flower only for a short time, whether they are deadheaded or not. For these plants, deadheading is a way to keep them looking their best by removing faded flowers.

Some plants have insignificant flowers and are grown only for their foliage. Coleus, caladium and polka-dot plant (*Hypoestes* species) are examples. If the flowers are removed, the plant's energy goes to producing a full, bushy plant. Deadheading is not appropriate if the plant you are growing has decorative seed heads, naturally. Love-in-a-mist (*Nigella damascena*) and starflower (*Scabiosa stellata*) are two plants grown for the beauty of their seedpods.

In the case of some impatiens and vinca (*Catharanthus roseus*), for example, flower production doesn't slow as they go to seed, so deadheading is unnecessary. But if you have the time, most flowering plants look better with an occasional cleanup of dead blossoms. As for cutting flowers, the more you cut, the more flowers the plants will produce.

Most plants grow more vigorously nearer the tips of their branches. Pinching back of the tips to the first node will force the plant to send out more branches closer to its middle. Pinching is necessary when you find your plant becoming leggy and losing its shape. Hanging pots purchased in full growth from a nursery usually need extra attention of continuously pinching back their tips to keep

Removing spent blossoms will make for a more attractive plant and can prolong the bloom.

them in good shape all summer; they have a tendency to grow out, losing their bushy shape. By cutting them back and preventing them from sprawling, you give them a longer and more productive life. (Unfortunately, pinching comes easily to children but not adults. I've often wished I could redirect my children while they're in their pinching stage to pinch my plants rather than the neighbors' children.)

On impatiens, fuchsia, begonias and other long-blooming flowers, pinch the branch back to the next bud with your fingers to encourage other branches to start from inside the plant and not out on the ends. Plants can get leggy quickly, and leggy plants are unattractive and deteriorate rapidly. One solution is to move a leggy plant out of sight and give it a crew cut. It won't be attractive again for several weeks, but you will have saved its life and given it back its youth. Once it fills out, bring it back into the limelight.

Shearing, cutting back the top of some plants to a crew cut, will induce them to bloom again. Alyssum responds well to this treatment, although I prefer a ragged, more natural look to the flattop cut. Root pruning is a good practice to help keep container plants a dwarf size. It shouldn't be done more than once a year, and fewer than a third of the roots should be cut to help keep the plant in bounds.

PROPAGATION THROUGH CUTTINGS

Some plants slow to grow from seed are readily propagated through cuttings. In the fall, before your container plants are killed by frost, you can take cuttings to grow over the winter and plant outside again in the spring, or to use as houseplants. Some plants, Wandering Jew and strawberry geranium, for example (see page 60), root so easily that they can be started in a glass of water. This is not, however, a good way to grow a healthy root because later the cutting may have trouble adjusting to soil, and a plant can't grow in water alone. To grow from cuttings:

1. Cut a 3- to 4-inch piece of new, tender stem, making sure to cut ½ inch below a node—the place where two or more branches or leaves come together. Position of the cut determines whether the cutting will have sufficient food reserves in its tissues to sustain it until roots are produced.

2. Pinch off all but two sets of leaves to prevent wilting and to promote rooting for the plant. More than two sets makes it hard for the developing root to sustain the plant above them. Remove any flower or flower buds to prevent them from zapping the stem's energies. Most cuttings benefit from being dipped in a rooting hormone (unnecessary for geraniums) to speed the growth of healthy new roots.

3. Fill a tray or a cup with a moist, not soggy, rooting medium (sand and vermiculite are two). Make a hole in the medium with a pencil. This hole should be wider than the cutting stem to keep the stem from damage or from losing any of the hormone powder clinging to it when it is placed in the medium. Stand the stem up in the hole and gently push the rooting medium around it. Be sure to place the node under the medium; this is where the roots will form.

4. Cover the cutting and the tray or cup with clear plastic, or put the whole thing in a plastic bag and place in a warm spot. Enclosure keeps the atmosphere moist. Rooting is promoted by moisture and warmth, particularly bottom heat. Use the top of a refrigerator or a warm, not hot, radiator, or a cold frame in partial sun; full sun will scorch or burn the cutting.

5. Plants root at different speeds, and as long as your stems remain healthy, they are fine. If you see rot or mildew, separate the affecting stem from any other cuttings and discard it.

In northern climates the long-blooming tuberous begonia 'Belgian Hybrid-Red' can be brought indoors and hung in a sunny window for continued bloom.

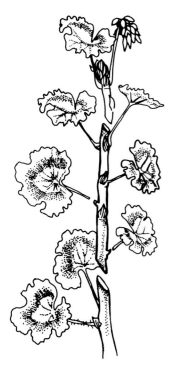

Make a cut about ½ inch below a node.

Gently firm the rooting medium around the stem.

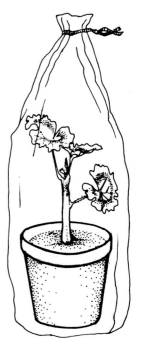

A clear plastic covering will ensure a moister environment for the cutting.

WINTER PROTECTION

Climates vary considerably from one end of our vast country to the other. The USDA's Plant Hardiness Map of the United States (page 92) is a gardener's guide to the average annual minimum temperatures in their part of the country. But zone charts referring to the hardiness of plants don't apply to container-grown plants. Because containers outdoors are exposed to the elements at the sides as well as the top, they dry out faster and need more frequent watering. For the same reason, container-grown plants are less winter-hardy than plants planted directly in the ground. Of course the more soil there is around tender roots, insulating them from freezing, the better. I asked expert gardeners in Zone 6 whether they left container-grown perennials, shrubs and evergreens outside unprotected for the winter. The answers varied wildly. In New York City alone, I talked with many landscape designers and landscape architects who completely wrapped plants of evergreens with Christmas-tree boughs or straw, secured with twine to hold them close to the container. Many others in the same area felt they didn't want to see evergreens shrouded for winter protection and were willing to risk foliage burn and, perhaps in an exceptionally cold winter, the loss of a plant. What became clear is that everyone's experience differs within even the same city block, depending on exposure to the sun and whether the garden in question is on a high-rise balcony or protected in a backyard. In Boston, Zone 5, many office buildings plant evergreens just as they plant summer annuals, knowing they will lose them at the end of the season but feeling it is a small price to pay for the lively greens that decorate and cheer during harsh winter weather.

It is a fact, however, that the soil in above-ground containers in Zones 5 and above can freeze solid, while this doesn't happen to roots below ground in the garden. Decks are more hostile to container plants than terraces because the air circulating under as well as above the plants will quickly freeze-burn the roots. Evergreens can be grown in containers in cold cli-

Houseplants vacationing outside for the summer decorate a window frame.

mates, Zone 5 and above, but they should either be brought into a protected area (garage, basement, greenhouse) for the winter or securely covered to protect them from the cold. Rocky Dale Nursery in coldest Vermont recommends consolidating containers in one area together, cheek to cheek, in close contact with the earth after the first hard frost or they have gone to sleep for the winter. They must be dormant when covered or they may rot. First cover the plants with a sheet of opaque plastic to keep the straw you're going to add from making a mess of the plants. Straw is then mounded on top of the plastic on all sides and on the top of the containers to a depth of at least a food. (Evergreen boughs or branches of Christmas trees can be substituted for the straw.) Another plastic sheet is placed on top of this and anchored down. The idea

is to insulate the plants from the hostile winter climate.

In milder climates, Zones 7 and 8, containers with evergreens and perennials don't need to be protected as a prolonged cold freezing the soil to 20° F or below is unlikely. The more tender plants can be protected temporarily with newspapers or plastic sheets if an exceptional cold spell is expected. All plants left uncovered will benefit from mulch on top of the soil to help conserve moisture. Broadleaf evergreens and needle-leaved evergreens need moisture throughout the winter. If rains are scarce the gardener should water every week or two. Broadleaf evergreens are especially susceptible to shriveling during winter as their leaves continue to release moisture into the air. If their soil is dry or frozen on the surface it prevents them from replacing needed moisture; the leaves shrivel and the plant may

die. In mild winter climates moist soil can act to insulate the roots against extreme cold and keep the plant from shriveling. To prevent drying out of broadleaf evergreens, spray the leaves with an antitranspirant, such as Wilt-Pruf or Cloud Cover. They coat the surface of the leaves and slow down transpiration without inhibiting photosynthesis. Antitranspirants are available at nurseries; because they are all a little different, it is important to follow the manufacturer's directions carefully.

Container gardening doesn't have to stop when Jack Frost chases you indoors. One of the best features of container gardening for northern gardeners is being able to move some of the flowers indoors before the first frost, thus bringing summer into the home and extending it well into fall and winter. Many plants can live as houseplants for the winter, moving back outdoors for their summer vacation.

It is safer to bring containers in before the first frost, although usually the first frost settles on the ground and not on hanging plants or plants close to the house. If the plants are brought in several weeks before frost and before fall's extreme contrasts of cold night temperatures and warm day temperatures, the plants will adjust better to indoor living. Their adjustment will be less traumatic. If you wait until right before the first frost, the hours of daylight will have shortened and the night temperatures dropped, increasing the contrast between the two. When you move a plant indoors it will again have to adjust to even day and night temperatures. When the temperature differences are extreme, plants frequently drop some leaves.

Some plants require a rest over the winter. After the plants stop blooming, cut back on the amount of water they receive and don't fertilize again until spring. Many summer-blooming bulbs can be removed from their pots and saved over the winter in a cool, dry place, then replanted in the spring. Dahlias, caladiums, calla lilies, canna lilies, gladiolus, gloriosa lilies, gloxinas and tuberous begonias store food in their roots over the summer. At summer's end the tuber will have increased in size. For most summer bulbs, after the first light frost or when frost has blackened your plants, cut the foliage back to within 1 to 6 inches of the soil (depending on the size of the plant). Very tender bulbs such as glorisoa lily and gloxinia should be moved to a shady, cool, dry place and water gradually withheld, allowing their foliage to die off and forcing the bulbs into dormancy. They will be damaged if left outdoors until hit by frost. Carefully unpot the plants, shake off the soil, and turn the plants upside down, to drain out excess moisture. Dry the tubers in a warm place for three to four hours, or if necessary, a few days, until they are dry to the touch. If you want to increase your stock of tubers, you may divide the clumps in the spring. Gladiolus are an exception and old corms should be discarded, as only the new corms formed each year will bloom the following year. Pack the tubers carefully in flats, boxes or bags and cover them with vermiculite, perlite, sand or granular peat to prevent them from shriveling during storage. Boxes should be stored in a frost-free, well-ventilated place with a temperature of 40° to 50° F. Check the tubers occasionally over the winter to make sure they remain plump. A light sprinkling of water may be needed once or twice throughout the winter. Should rotting occur, discard bad tubers and provide better ventilation and perhaps a cooler temperature. Plant in the spring, either starting them indoors early or outdoors after all chance of frost is past.

Geraniums also can be kept dormant over the winter. As flowering slows, water should be gradually withheld and stems cut back to a few inches in height. Store in a cool, dark place. They need minimal water every four to six weeks, and no fertilizer, during their dormant period. They can be removed from their pots and stored with the soil left on their roots, or they can be left in their pots. Replant in the spring. As the plants begin to sprout new leaves, add water and fertilizer gradually. Move the plants slowly, over a period of weeks, into an area with more light, and finally to a sunny window.

Containers too large to be moved can be covered with heavy sheets of plastic. Tie the plastic securely in place to keep water from collecting inside, freezing and breaking the container. One lazy fall, I covered a large terra-cotta planter with heavy clear plastic without removing the summer annuals. Removing the plastic after a mild winter, I was surprised to find several of the scented geraniums and vincas had survived the winter only slightly damaged, with brown tips on some leaves. The plastic acted like a cold frame. This won't happen every year, but it is certainly worth a try for gardeners in Zone 7.

5

PESTS AND DISEASES

Good gardening calls for observation and understanding. Close observation of your plants will make it more likely you'll detect problems early, and early detection will help you check a disease or keep an insect from doing great damage. A curled leaf, for example, may be a sign the plant is too dry, has an insect problem or nitrogen deficiency, or that a fungus has attacked. If you don't immediately know what is causing the problem, a closer look is warranted.

It is a good idea to inspect your plants with a magnifying glass at the first signs of trouble. A magnifying glass will take the guesswork out of identifying your plant's problem. Many insects such as spider mites and aphids are difficult to see. Check the undersides of the leaves, where they like to hide. Spider mites are almost impossible to see, but if you hold a piece of white paper under the leaves and shake the stem, red specks will show up on the paper. Plant pests don't have to be big to be damaging. Early detection and prevention are the keys to good health—for all living things.

Understanding each plant's needs will help prevent problems before they start. Whether a plant has an unquenchable thirst and likes its feet wet, or perfers to let the soil dry out completely between waterings, is important information for the health of your plant. If you notice a plant looking a little peeked, don't sit and watch it go downhill, do something. Perhaps it needs protection from the wind, more sun or a little shade. While there are general guidelines for plant care, there are always exceptions. Learn to treat each plant as an individual. Read about its likes and dislikes, its family history, its origin (see page 43).

Keeping plants clean is important for their good health. Dusty or dirty leaves keep sun from the plant, retard transpiration and invite fungus and disease to settle in. Container plants that are not placed where rains will cleanse them need to be hosed or washed weekly. On city balconies and backyards where air pollution from traffic is high, more frequent washing is necessary. A diluted solution of gentle liquid dishwashing soap can be used. It will not only clean the leaves but will stop many diseases and fungi in their early stages.

When watering your plants pick off dead flowers and yellowed leaves and check the undersides of the leaves for disease and insects. Remove any dead branches; this is one place disease can start, and if you don't check closely, the disease could be rampant before it's noticeable on the outside branches. Carefully check between the branches of plants with dense growth for any signs of furry mealybugs, crawling aphids and jumping white flies.

A diseased container plant can be isolated from other plants—not a luxury plants growing out in the garden share. If treatment requires spraying, the plant can be put in a plastic bag (or a dry-cleaning bag, if the plant is large) before spraying, so the spray is contained; don't leave the bag on the plant for more than a few hours, especially on hot days, or you may suffocate it.

The common garden problems of soil-borne

A raised bed in the center of this terrace is surrounded by many gardens. The sides of the raised bed are high enough to support tomatoes growing down over the edges. This is easier and more attractive than growing tomatoes in cages or staking them. Red tomatoes are decorative, and off the ground the fruit stays clean and easy to pick.

diseases and insects, and even overwatering, shouldn't exist in a container if you use a well-drained sterile soil. But don't be fooled into thinking there won't be challenges or problems. Even if you garden twenty stories up, somehow pests and diseases will find your garden. I recently noticed a small snail at the top of a mammoth, 12-foot sunflower. Imagine the energy, time and determination he needed to reach that height. Why he did it when surrounding the sunflower, at ground level, was a vegetable garden that would feed a small army, I don't know. (That snail is more persistent than I will ever be.) This is yet another example of the challenges of living with plants, although from another perspective than mine.

Our preference at Burpee has always been for the natural controls. We have all watched chemicals come onto the market, touted as the miracle control for this or that pest or disease, only later to learn the chemicals endanger our environment. In some cases, after many years, we watched as more resilient bugs appeared, no longer controlled by the same chemicals. Chemicals do kill pests for a time, but they harm the beneficial insects that nature has provided for a balanced environment too. So, at Burpee we work with nature first and use chemicals only when all else has failed. With carefully selected disease-resistant plants, chemicals should almost never be needed. Still, on rare occasions, even the best-cared-for gardens have problems. Here are some of the ways you can work to prevent problems, as well as identify and treat them early.

CAUTION: Petrochemical pesticides require care in use. If you have occasion to use them, respect their proper handling at all times, including storage. Accidents from poorly stored pesticides are too common. Keep them out of reach of children and well covered, and always follow the manufacturer's instructions carefully. Never spray or use chemicals with children or animals around.

Warfare: Chemical or Natural?

If a plant needs chemicals to grow in your garden, ask yourself: "Do I really need this plant?" The instant cure that chemicals promise is misleading. Make sure you understand the side effects from chemicals. Chemicals linger in the soil, seeping deep into and contaminating ground water. When sprayed on plants, they kill beneficial and harmful insects and bacteria alike. The easier, safer and healthier cure is one in concert with Mother Nature and the environment.

Use garden netting or row covers to keep large insects off container-grown crops. Biodegradable products made by Safer's, Inc., and Ringer's safely do the job of petrochemical-based insecticides and fungicides. Always try these before resorting to toxic products. Some old-fashioned remedies work well too. A spray of two tablespoons vinegar or one tablespoon baking soda to one gallon of water makes an effective treatment for mold and powdery mildew. If you need more help or have a very severe problem, it is best to consult your county extension service for the most up-to-date information on controls for your area.

DISEASES

Botrytis

Another name for botrytis is "gray mold blight," a pretty good description of what to look for. Caused by humid conditions, it can be controlled by good air circulation, good sanitation and prompt removal of any plant's diseased part to avoid spreading. Safer's™ Garden Fungicide can be used as a preventive.

Leaf Spot

This occurs most often in humid or wet weather and may be the result of bacteria or fungus. Spots of color (red, brown, yellow) appear on foliage. Sometimes, as they dry, the spots drop out, leaving holes. Remove the infected foliage to avoid spreading the disease, which is transmitted by rain, dew, soil, seeds and gardeners. Keep the plants moist but not wet, and avoid overhead watering. Don't work in a wet garden, especially with diseased plants; this is when the disease is most likely to be spread. A fungicide will not be effective on foliage affected by bacteria.

Powdery Mildew

When powdery mildew is present the plants look like they are covered with a dirty white dust. Not only is it unattractive but it causes leaves to curl and dry out, and buds to die before blooming. By giving plants good air circulation, and watering only in the morning—directly into the container without wetting the foliage—problems can be kept to a minimum. However, some plants, such as garden phlox, are extremely susceptible. Safer's™ Garden Fungicide is a good preventive that doesn't leave a noticeable residue. Look for plant varieties that are disease resistant.

Rust

Cool, damp nights and humid days encourage rust. Rust is visible in raised and discolored (yellow, reddish or orange) spots that appear on the undersides or leaves, causing them to wither. Don't overwater, avoid overhead watering and remove infected leaves. Look for rust-resistant varieties of your favorite plants; resistance to rust should be indicated on the seed packet.

Wilt

Wilt may have more than one cause. It can be a physiological problem, whereby plants wilt from lack of water in the soil, or it can be a pathological problem, caused by fungi plugging up the water-conducting tissue in the roots and stems of the plants. The symptoms are the same: a droopy plant with downward-curling leaves. If the problem is physiological, the water-conducting channels in the leaves and the stem quit working and go limp. The plant will recover and regain its stiffness when watered—unless it has been dry too long To avoid this problem, water your plants regularly and deeply, and fertilize them to promote vigorous growth.

When the problem is pathological, caused by a fungus disease also called "wilt," the plants can't recover, even when watered, because the water-conducting tissues are plugged forever. When buying seeds or plants, choose varities that are wilt resistant (resistant to the fungus, that is—no plant is resistant to being too dry).

PESTS

Aphids

Their method of damaging plants is similar to the spider mites' but, in addition, when they suck from the plant they can introduce infection and spread disease. Aphids are soft-bodied, pear-shaped and multicolored. Although they are quite small, they're usually not difficult to see because they arrive in mobs. A strong spray of water or an organic insecticide will help to dispel and destroy them.

Beetles

There are many different kinds of beetles (Mexican bean beetle, Japanese beetle, flea beetle,

Aphids

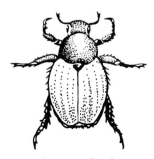
Japanese Beetle

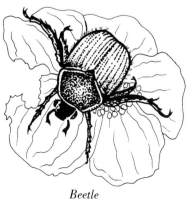
Beetle

Leafhopper

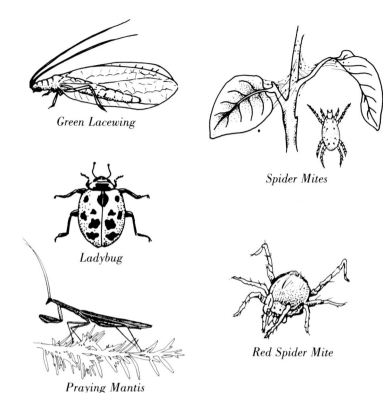

Green Lacewing

Ladybug

Spider Mites

Red Spider Mite

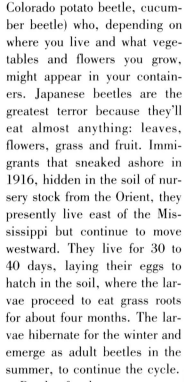

Praying Mantis

Colorado potato beetle, cucumber beetle) who, depending on where you live and what vegetables and flowers you grow, might appear in your containers. Japanese beetles are the greatest terror because they'll eat almost anything: leaves, flowers, grass and fruit. Immigrants that sneaked ashore in 1916, hidden in the soil of nursery stock from the Orient, they presently live east of the Mississippi but continue to move westward. They live for 30 to 40 days, laying their eggs to hatch in the soil, where the larvae proceed to eat grass roots for about four months. The larvae hibernate for the winter and emerge as adult beetles in the summer, to continue the cycle.

Beetles for the most part are slow moving and easily can be flicked off the leaves into a jar half filled with water where they will drown. Natural insecticides are available that can be sprayed on the plants. For the squeamish, a beetle trap that lures male beetles with a powerful sex lure, female beetles with a floral lure, can be hung a distance from the containers. (Placed near the containers, it will only attract more beetles to your plants.) The beetles that enter the trap die there. Beetles can

and should additionally be treated while in their grub stage. Ringer's Grub Attack kills by infecting Japanese beetle grubs with milky spore disease, caused by *bacillus popilliae*, a natural ingredient. Grubs stop feeding and die, releasing billions of new spores to kill other grubs. A single application continues to work for 10 or more years.

Leafhoppers

Wedge-shaped, small and green, gray or yellow in color, leafhoppers suck juices from the plant and leave it with discolored yellow leaves, stunted growth and buds that do not blossom. They are also carriers of plant diseases, particularly yellows.

Ladybugs, green lacewings and praying mantises love leafhoppers for dinner. All these insects can be purchased through

the mail from Burpee and released at the base of your containers. An insecticidal soap used early in the day, when the leafhoppers are less active, will rid the plant of them. It is best to use the soap every few days until the pests are gone.

Mites

Eight-legged and borderline microscopic, mites are easily located by their webs on the undersides of leaves. Mites suck moisture and chlorophyll from the leaves, leaving them yellow and wrinkled.

If you discover tiny red spots on the underside of your leaves, your plant doesn't have the measles. It's an attack of spider mites. Wash affected plants with a strong spray of cold water or spray with an organic insecticide to help control them. Safer's insecticidal soap is best, but 2 tablespoons of dishwashing liquid can be mixed with a gallon of water and used, if washed away completely after treatment to avoid damaging the leaves. Repeat every few days until problem mites are gone.

Ladybugs are spider mites' natural enemies. They can be purchased through the Burpee catalogue and released on your plants.

A forceful spray of water directed weekly at the underside of the leaves will control the mites.

Whiteflies

Whiteflies grow to 1/16 inch and have very large white wings for their size. They suck the plant leaves, which turn yellow and eventually fall off. Yellow pests strips coated with oil attract whiteflies; the whiteflies stick to them and can't move. This is a fairly effective and pleasant way to control numbers of this pest if you manage to hang the strips discreetly out of sight. A good breeze will blow the pests away, too.

Slugs and Snails

If they were entered side by side in a beauty contest, the snails would win because their ugly slimy, wormlike bodies are hidden by shells. Snails and slugs behave alike, coming out at night or after a rain to devour foliage. They live in mulch and garden waste and have no trouble climbing the sides of planters to reach the plants. The brave can pick them off and squash or step on them. The rest of us simply need to spread diatomaceous earth (ground fossilized aquatic plants, commercially available in bags) around the bases of plants. Slugs and snails avoid crawling through rough soil, which scratches and tears their smooth skin.

Leaves damaged by the following pests, from left: beetles, flea beetles, caterpillars, aphids and leafminers.

Whiteflies

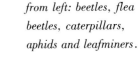

Snail

Slug

6

GARDENERS' MOST-ASKED QUESTIONS

The first Burpee catalog was mailed in 1876, and catalogs have been coming ever since, offering gardeners a wealth of seeds, plants, fruits, shrubs and trees, as well as advice for better gardening. From the early years to today, Burpee has received many letters from customers describing their gardens and asking for advice. Here are the most frequently asked questions Burpee receives about container gardening.

SHADE

Q: I live in a city apartment with a balcony. Can I grow anything in a container when I have shade most of the day?
A: There are many plants, even with brightly colored flowers, for growing in the shade. For a peaceful place to sit above the noise of the city, grow plants that suggest a woodland setting: ferns, hostas, azaleas, caladiums and ivy. Consider the houseplants that bloom in dim indoor light and the bulbs and annuals that bloom in shady conditions, too. The only category of plants difficult to grow in the shade is vegetables. However, lettuce and leafy greens will tolerate a half-day of sun (see Winning Combinations for Containers in Shade, pages 40–41).

PLANTING

Q: Can I plant annuals more closely in containers than the recommended spacing?
A: Yes, in fact, I recommend it. Plants generally grow smaller in containers because they don't have the room to stretch their legs. In a container, water and fertilizer must be regularly applied so your plants will not have to fight each other for their nutrients as they might in the garden. For more information about fertilizer, see page 74.

Q: How many plants can I put in a container?
A: Always plant more closely in a container than you would in a garden. Containers need to be fully packed, hiding the soil, to look their best. When you are transplanting seedlings or young plants, the size of their existing roots will show you how many you can easily plant together, giving them room to grow. If they become too crowded, one or more plants can be transplanted to another pot. Roots automatically grow downward (provided the container is deep enough), and container plants can "get by" this way—they won't need as much space between individuals.

Burpee employees filling orders in 1907.

WATER GARDEN

Q: Can I have a water garden in a container?

A: Many water-gardening supply companies and nurseries sell all the equipment necessary for growing waterlilies and other small aquatic plants in containers. Some have even come with a pump for circulating the water, to keep it clean. An inexpensive wooden half barrel can be lined with plastic to hold water. Potted miniature waterlilies can be placed in the barrel, raised to the proper level on top of bricks or an inverted pot. Most waterlilies prefer that the rim of their pot be several inches below the water level to allow the plants to grow up and float on the surface. If the tub will not be recycling and filtering water, add fish, snails and oxygenating plants, such as anacharis, to help keep the water clean by absorbing water impurities and freeing oxygen.

PLANTS FOR PARTIAL SHADE (FOUR HOURS OF DIRECT SUN PER DAY)

COMMON NAME	LATIN NAME	COMMON NAME	LATIN NAME
Ageratum	*Ageratum houstonianum*	Ground ivy	*Glechoma hederacea*
Asparagus fern	*Asparagus densiflorus*	Heliotrope	*Heliotropium* species
Azalea	*Rhododendron* species	Impatiens	*Impatiens* species
Beefsteak plant	*Perilla* species	Ivy	*Hedera* species
Begonia	*Begonia* species	Japanese painted fern	*Athyrium niponicum pictum*
Bells of Ireland	*Molucella* species		
Browallia	*Browallia* species	Lady fern	*Athyrium filix-femina*
Caladium	*Caladium* species	Lisianthus	*Eustoma grandiflorum*
Camellia	*Camellia* species	Lobelia	*Lobelia erinus*
Christmas fern	*Polystichum acrostichoides*	Monkey flower	*Mimulus* species
Cockscomb	*Celosia* species	Nasturtium	*Tropaeolum* species
Crocus	*Crocus* species	Pansy	*Viola* species
Cupflower	*Nierembergia caerulea*	Pellionia	*Pellionia pulchra*
Daffodil	*Narcissus* species	Periwinkle	*Catharanthus roseus*
Dahlia	*Dahlia* species	Polka-dot plant	*Hypoestes* species
Farewell-to-spring	*Clarkia amoena*	Spider plant	*Cleome* species
Flowering maple	*Abutilon* species	Snowdrop	*Leucojum* species
Flowering tobacco	*Nicotiana* species	Strawberry geranium	*Saxifraga stolonifera*
Foliage plant	*Coleus* species	Sunflower	*Helianthus* species
Forget-me-not	*Myosotis sylvatica*	Swedish ivy	*Plectranthus australis*
Four-o'clock	*Mirabilis* species	Sweet alyssum	*Lobularia maritima*
Funkia	*Hosta* species	Velvet flower	*Salpiglossis* species
Geranium	*Pelargonium* species	Wishbone flower	*Torenia fournieri*
Grape ivy	*Cissus rhombifolia* 'Ellen Danica'		

SEEDS

Q: Can I start seeds right in the pot where the mature plant will grow?

A: Yes. Many vegetables and annuals benefit from being sown directly in the pot and not suffering the trauma of transplanting. Follow the directions on the back of individual seed packages. Many varieties of vegetables and flowers can be started earlier indoors under lights or in a sunny window and moved out when all danger of frost is past. Garden blankets, a little-known asset to the gardener, are made from a synthetic fabric and can be fitted over the top of the pot to help speed germination for those plants started outdoors. Garden blankets protect the plants from cool nights while allowing air, water and 75 to 80 percent of the natural sunlight to pass through. In addition they hold the heat and moisture, raising the soil temperature and preventing newly sown seeds from washing away in rain. Garden blankets are available through the Burpee catalog and at your local nursery. Take advantage of the mobility of containers and move them into optimum positions for quicker growth.

GROWING

Q: Should containers be raised a few inches above the surface on which they stand, even if the container has drainage holes?

A: It is always best to raise a container off the ground to prevent the base of the container from sitting in the water that can collect in the bottom of the pot or a saucer under the pot. Saucers can hold several inches of water, enough to drown and rot the bottom roots. Plants can be raised on top of inverted pots, plant stands and bricks. Decorative iron feet and pedestals are also available.

Q: Do I have to repot container plants every year?

A: It depends on the plant and its environment. Each variety grows at a different pace. Some plants, such as clivia, prefer their roots crowded and will bloom the better for it; others will stop blooming when overcrowded. Many plants, including lots of perennials, can be divided to increase your number of plants, and when repotting is the perfect time to do this.

Q: How can I tell when it is time to transplant to a larger container?

A: A sparsely flowering plant may need transplanting. If the roots are growing out of the bottom hole the plant could use a larger pot. Exposed roots around the top of the pot and pressing against the sides are another sign the plant needs repotting. (If you are unsure, remove the plant and check the roots.) The roots will have to be loosened and gently forced to grow out into the soil of the larger pot. If the roots continue to grow in a circle inside the new pot, they will constrict the plant's growth. If they don't fill the new pot, the plant can be replaced easily in its original pot. Repotting is an opportunity to improve the soil, necessary if it is compact or forms a hard crust on the surface.

OVERWINTERING CONTAINERS

Q: How can I overwinter hardy plants in containers?

A: In the most northern gardens, the coldest parts of Zone 6 and north, it is best to bring the plants indoors for the winter. A garage, a basement, a greenhouse, a sun porch and a laundry room all will be appropriate if the plant gets light and is kept at cool temperatures. In northern gardens where winter temperatures drop below freezing but stay above 20° F, plant hardy plants in unbreakable containers. Terra-cotta pots can be wrapped with wire under the rim for extra support, to prevent breakage in milder northern climates.

For protection from strong winds, barricades of burlap can be placed around the plants. Straw or evergreen branches can be laid on top of the soil and around the plants to keep the soil from quickly freezing, then thawing, which can force a plant out of its pot; it will protect against prolonged freezing, too, which can burn the roots. A piece of old garden hose or plastic drainage pipe can be plugged at each end (to prevent soil from getting inside), then buried in the pot. If the pots freeze, the expanding soil will press against the flexible hose or pipe, compressing the air inside the hose; this will relieve the pressure on the outside of the pot and save it from possible breakage. If possible, move the container to a more protected place, next to a wall or in a corner.

Even in winter plants need water. It might be necessary on a warm winter day to water your container. In southern gardens where frost is rare, a garden blanket, heavy plastic sheet or layers of newspaper can be placed over the plants when frost is expected and removed after all danger is past. See pages 50–51 for information on protecting perennials, pages 77–78 for shrubs and evergreens.

TREES

Q: Which trees can be grown in containers?
A: The size of the container—and the growing area available above it—will help determine the size and height of the tree. Trees in containers don't grow as large as they would if planted in the ground, where their roots can grow out as they will. Many dwarf trees can be grown in a pot with a depth of 2½ feet. Deciduous trees (those that lose their leaves in fall or winter) grown in containers in areas with heavy frost will need to be protected or brought in for winter; if the container freezes solid, the tree will die.

VEGETABLES

Q: How large a container do I need to grow tomatoes? Bush cucumbers? Peppers?
A: For tomatoes, it depends on the type. Tomato 'Pixie Hybrid II' is a small bush tomato with medium-sized fruits that can be grown in an 8- by 8-inch container. It tops out at an average of 18 inches tall, with tomatoes 2 inches across. The advantage of this variety is that if grown outdoors in the summer, tomatoes will ripen in just over 50 days. (It can also be grown indoors on a windowsill in winter, but will take longer to ripen with the shorter days of winter.) Most other tomatoes require a container at least 12 by 12 inches, with supports for the plants.

Bush cucumbers and peppers can also be planted singly or several to each 12- by 12-inch container, depending on the variety. When you purchase seeds or started plants, note the spacing recommendations. As long as you provide a soil depth of 12 inches and fertilize regularly, you can space the plants several inches closer together than is recommended for planting out in the garden. Plants tend to grow smaller in containers than in a garden. See the chart on page 46 for other vegetables and their required container size.

VINES

Q: Can I grow vines in containers? How should they be supported?

A: Vines are ideal plants for large containers. Most vines have deep roots and need a minimum soil depth of 12 inches to support the growth of long stems. Supports for vines will be stronger if they are attached to the containers, but poles and trellises can be anchored into the soil. Containers can have vines sprawling over their sides or growing up walls, trellises, railings or poles.

Please write or call for a free Burpee catalog:
W. Atlee Burpee & Company
300 Park Avenue
Warminster, PA 18974
215-674-9633

THE USDA
PLANT
HARDINESS
MAP
OF THE
UNITED
STATES

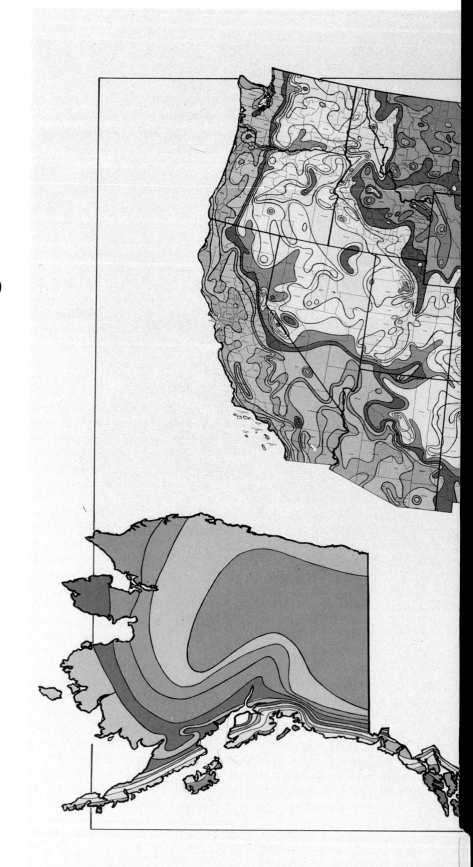

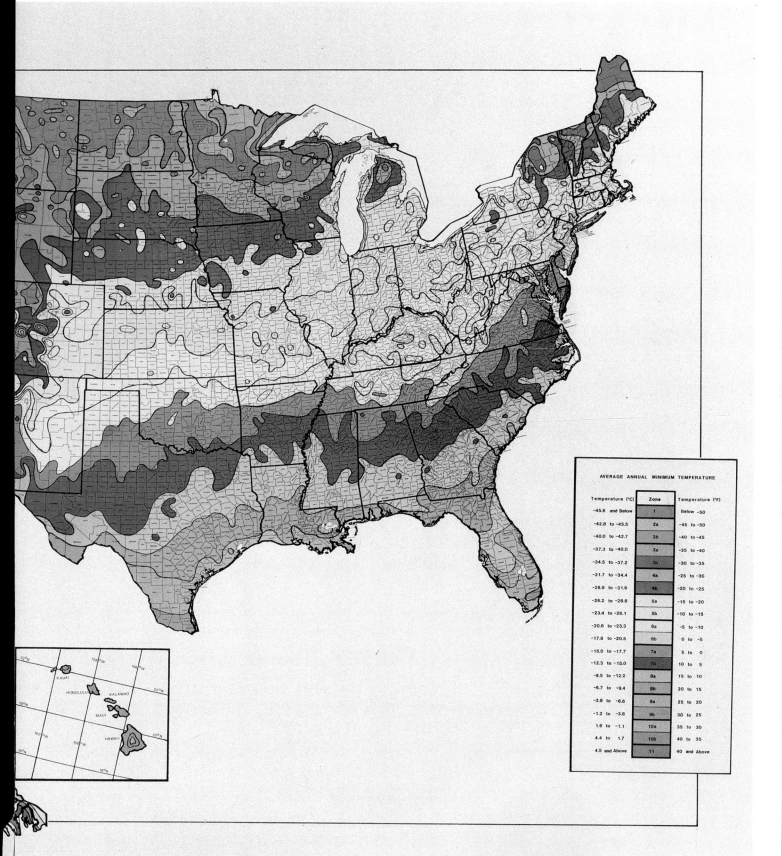

AVERAGE ANNUAL MINIMUM TEMPERATURE

Temperature (°C)	Zone	Temperature (°F)
−45.6 and Below	1	Below −50
−42.8 to −45.5	2a	−45 to −50
−40.0 to −42.7	2b	−40 to −45
−37.3 to −40.0	3a	−35 to −40
−34.5 to −37.2	3b	−30 to −35
−31.7 to −34.4	4a	−25 to −30
−28.9 to −31.6	4b	−20 to −25
−26.2 to −28.8	5a	−15 to −20
−23.4 to −26.1	5b	−10 to −15
−20.6 to −23.3	6a	−5 to −10
−17.8 to −20.5	6b	0 to −5
−15.0 to −17.7	7a	5 to 0
−12.3 to −15.0	7b	10 to 5
−9.5 to −12.2	8a	15 to 10
−6.7 to −9.4	8b	20 to 15
−3.9 to −6.6	9a	25 to 20
−1.2 to −3.8	9b	30 to 25
1.6 to −1.1	10a	35 to 30
4.4 to 1.7	10b	40 to 35
4.5 and Above	11	40 and Above

INDEX

Italicized page numbers refer to captions.